REVISE BTEC TECH AWARD
Sport, Activity and Fitness

REVISION GUIDE

Series Consultant: Harry Smith

Author: Jennifer Stafford-Brown

While the publishers have made every attempt to ensure that advice on the qualification and its assessment is accurate, the official specification and associated assessment guidance materials are the only authoritative source of information and should always be referred to for definitive guidance.

This qualification is reviewed on a regular basis and may be updated in the future. Any such updates that affect the content of this Revision Guide will be outlined at www.pearsonfe.co.uk/BTECchanges. The eBook version of this Revision Guide will also be updated to reflect the latest guidance as soon as possible.

For the full range of Pearson revision titles across KS2, KS3, GCSE, Functional Skills, AS/A Level and BTEC visit:
www.pearsonschools.co.uk/revise

Published by Pearson Education Limited, 80 Strand, London, WC2R ORL.

www.pearsonschoolsandfecolleges.co.uk

Copies of official specifications for all Pearson qualifications may be found on the website: qualifications.pearson.com

Text and illustrations © Pearson Education Ltd 2019
Typeset and illustrated by QBS Learning
Produced by QBS Learning
Cover illustration by Clementine Hope

The right of Jennifer Stafford-Brown to be identified as author of this work has been asserted by her in accordance with the Copyright, Designs and Patents Act 1988.

First published 2019

22 21 20 19
10 9 8 7 6 5 4 3 2 1

British Library Cataloguing in Publication Data
A catalogue record for this book is available from the British Library

ISBN 978 1 292 32786 0

Printed in Slovakia by Neografia

Acknowledgements
Text credits:

5: Robert Davis et al. Extract from *Physical Education and Study of Sport*, fourth edition, 978 0 723 43175 6, © 2000, Elsevier.

Photographs: (Key: t: top; b: bottom; c: centre; l: left; r: right)

Alamy Stock Photo: Rupert Rivett iii, 20, B Christopher 33, Leithan Partnership t/a The Picture Pantry 34, Editorial Image LLC 41bl, Cultura Creative (RF) 44, Andrew Lloyd 45, Andrew Orchard Sports Photography 47, **Getty Images:** Andrey Popov/iStock 10, FatCamera/E+ 12t, 18, Caiaimage/Sam Edwards 12b, Abezikus/iStock 14, FlamingoImages/iStock 19cl, Avid_creative/E+ 19cr, Digital Vision 22bl, Caiaimage/Sam Edwards 22cr, Kyoshino/E+ 34, Russell Sadur/Dorling Kindersley 37, Geber86/E+ 38, Westend61 39, NoirChocolate/iStock 41tl, MentalArt/iStock 41br, SolStock/E+ 43, Koji Aoki 48, **Shutterstock:** Robert Kneschke 1,49, Stephen Mcsweeny 5, Watchares Hansawek 6, Stefan Schurr 8, Christopher Elwell 13, Mangpor2004 15, Konstantin Sutyagin 16, Maridav 17, Kameel4u 23, Iakov Filimonov 24, Maanas 27, Bobex-73 30, ESB Professional 35, Alexander Raths 36, Diana Taliun 41tr, NaturalBox 41bc, Andrey Popov 46.

Notes from the publisher
1. While the publishers have made every attempt to ensure that advice on the qualification and its assessment is accurate, the official specification and associated assessment guidance materials are the only authoritative source of information and should always be referred to for definitive guidance.

Pearson examiners have not contributed to any sections in this resource relevant to examination papers for which they have responsibility.

2. Pearson has robust editorial processes, including answer and fact checks, to ensure the accuracy of the content in this publication, and every effort is made to ensure this publication is free of errors. We are, however, only human, and occasionally errors do occur. Pearson is not liable for any misunderstandings that arise as a result of errors in this publication, but it is our priority to ensure that the content is accurate. If you spot an error, please do contact us at resourcescorrections@pearson.com so we can make sure it is corrected.

Websites
Pearson Education Limited is not responsible for the content of any external internet sites. It is essential for tutors to preview each website before using it in class so as to ensure that the URL is still accurate, relevant and appropriate. We suggest that tutors bookmark useful websites and consider enabling students to access them through the school/college intranet.

Introduction

Revising Component 2 of your BTEC Tech Award

This Revision Guide has been designed to support you in preparing for the externally assessed component of your course.

The assessment for Component 2, The Principles of Training, Nutrition and Psychology for Sport and Activity, is in the form of a paper comprising short, long and extended writing questions. This will be completed under supervised conditions in a specified time. This assessment is likely to take place towards the end of your course. You will be expected to link knowledge and understanding with the other components. In particular, you will use the knowledge and understanding of this component in Component 3.

Your Revision Guide

Each unit in this Revision Guide contains two types of pages, shown below.

Content pages help you revise the essential content you need to know for each unit.

Skills pages help you prepare for your exam or assessed task. Skills pages have a coloured edge and are shaded in the table of contents.

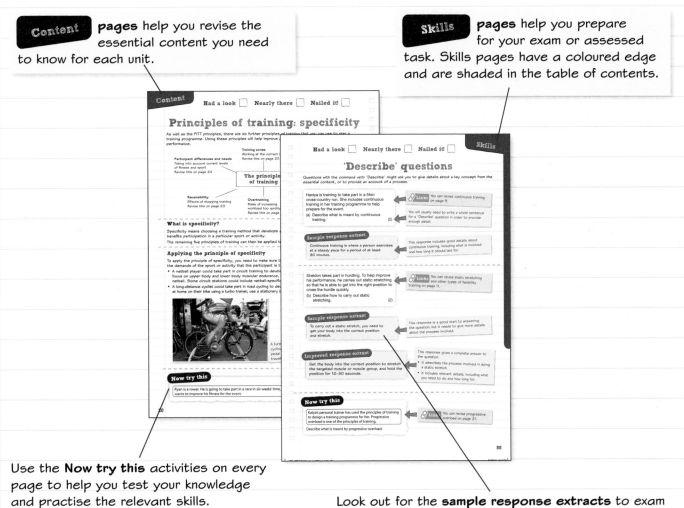

Use the **Now try this** activities on every page to help you test your knowledge and practise the relevant skills.

Look out for the **sample response extracts** to exam questions or set tasks on the skills pages. Post-its will explain their strengths and weaknesses.

Contents

. . . .

A small bit of small print
Pearson publishes Sample Assessment Material and the Specification on its website. This is the official content and this book should be used in conjunction with it. The questions in *Now try this* have been written to help you test your knowledge and skills. Remember: the real assessment may not look like this.

Fitness testing

Fitness is an overall term covering seven different components. Different types of fitness test are carried out to provide measurements of each component of fitness.

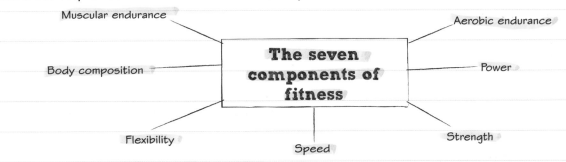

The seven components of fitness

- Muscular endurance
- Aerobic endurance
- Body composition
- Power
- Flexibility
- Speed
- Strength

Fitness tests

Tests have been designed to measure each component of fitness. The results are used to find out which components of fitness are a person's strengths and which components need to be developed.

Each test needs specific equipment. The person carrying out the test needs to follow a **protocol**, which is the set method of administering the test.

The protocol includes information on:

1. how the test should be set up

2. which equipment should be used

3. how to complete the test correctly

4. how to record the results accurately.

Fitness programmes can be developed which maintain a person's strengths and develop weaker components.

Interpreting fitness test results

Fitness test results are interpreted by comparing an individual's results with the published **normative data** for other people of the same age group and gender.

- This shows whether an individual has lower or higher results than most of the population.
- The normative data tables are produced by calculating the average scores from fitness test results.

Normative data

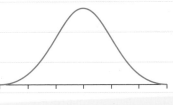

When people's measurements are plotted on a graph, they form a shape like this. Most people's results are in the middle of the curve.

Age	Excellent	Above average
13–14	>2700 m	2400–2700 m
15–16	>2900 m	2500–2800 m
17–19	>3000 m	2700–3000 m
20–29	>2800 m	2400–2800 m
30–39	>2700 m	2300–2700 m
40–49	>2500 m	2100–2500 m
>50	>2400 m	2000–2400 m

Part of a table showing normative data for male athletes

Now try this

1 Define what is meant by a fitness test protocol.

2 Describe why a normative data graph is highest in the middle.

3 Identify the two different groups of people that normative data tables can be produced for.

1

Aerobic endurance

Aerobic endurance is also known as cardiovascular fitness. This component of fitness is used when taking part in physical activity at a moderate intensity for at least 30 minutes.

Importance of aerobic endurance

The greater a person's **aerobic endurance**, the more efficient their cardiorespiratory system in supplying nutrients and oxygen to their working muscles. This helps the person to continue participating in the activity, at the same intensity, for longer.

Sports and activities that require aerobic endurance

Sports where aerobic endurance is ...	
a key component of performance	part of the overall profile
• Cross-country running • Long-distance swimming • Cycling • Triathlon	• Racket sports • Team sports such as football and netball during periods of moderate intensity, as these games last more than 30 minutes.

Cooper 12-minute run test

This fitness test is used to measure aerobic endurance. It involves running for 12 minutes and the distance covered is recorded.

Equipment

Athletics track, cones, whistle, stop watch, tape measure.

Protocol

Before taking part in the test, the participant should carry out an appropriate warm-up (look at page 28 for warm-up routines).

1 The participant stands at the starting line on the athletics track.

2 Blow a whistle for the participant to start running around the track.

3 At 12 minutes, blow the whistle again for the participant to stop running.

4 Place a cone at the point where they stopped running.

5 Measure the distance covered and record it to the nearest 10 m.

Advantages and disadvantages

👍 This is a good test for people whose sport involves running, as the test involves the type of activity used in their sport.

👍 The test does not require much equipment and is easy to set up.

👍 A number of people can take part in the test at the same time.

👎 The test may not reflect the true aerobic endurance of people who do not run in their sport, such as swimmers.

👎 The running surface and climate can affect the **reliability** of this test. A slippery surface or a hot day can result in lower scores.

Reliability

Reliability refers to how similar the results would be if the test were repeated. When someone takes the test again, their results should remain the same or very similar, as long as their fitness levels haven't changed.

Normative test data

Age	Excellent	Above average	Average	Below average	Poor
13–14	>2000 m	1900–2000 m	1600–1899 m	1500–1599 m	>1500 m
15–16	>2100 m	2000–2100 m	1700–1999 m	1600–1699 m	>1600 m
17–20	>2300 m	2100–2300 m	1800–2099 m	1700–1799 m	>1700 m
20–29	>2700 m	2200–2700 m	1800–2199 m	1500–1799 m	>1500 m

Part of the normative data table for female athletes. There is also one available for male athletes. The complete table would also show age ranges 30–39, 40–49 and 50+ years.

Now try this

Molly is 16 years old and swims in long-distance races at county level. She achieves a distance of 1650m in the Cooper 12-minute run test.

1 Look at the normative data table for female athletes. Identify the category for Molly's result.

2 Explain if you think this score is a true reflection of Molly's aerobic endurance.

Muscular endurance

Muscular endurance is the ability of a muscle group to perform repeated contractions over an extended time.

Importance

Muscular endurance is required in everyday activities such as walking and climbing stairs.

It is a key component of fitness for many sports and activities where a participant must perform repeated movements at a low to moderate intensity.

Sports requiring good muscular endurance

Activities that require high levels of muscular endurance include repeated squats, pull-ups, press-ups and sit-ups.

Sports where muscular endurance is ...	
a key component of performance	part of the overall profile
• Distance running, cycling, swimming, rowing • Triathlon	• Racket sports • Team sports: football, netball, basketball, rugby

One-minute sit-up test

This test measures the muscular endurance of the abdominal muscles. The participant performs as many sit-ups as possible in one minute, using the correct technique. This test can be used to provide an overall indicator of a person's muscular endurance.

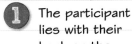 The participant lies with their back on the floor, fingers on their temples or crossed across their chest and knees bent. You can hold the participant's feet so that they remain on the ground.

② Say 'Go' and start the stop watch. The participant sits up until their elbows touch their knees.

③ They return to the start position with the back of their head touching the floor.

④ The participant does as many sit-ups as they can in one minute.

⑤ Say 'Stop' after one minute. Record the number of sit-ups completed.

Equipment	Protocol
Mat, stop watch.	Before doing the test, the participant should carry out an appropriate warm-up (look at page 28 for routines).

Normative test data

	Number of sit-ups	
Rating	Males	Females
Excellent	49–59	42–54
Good	43–48	37–41
Above average	39–42	32–36
Average	35–38	28–31
Below average	31–34	24–27
Poor	25–30	18–23
Very poor	11–24	3–17

A normative data table for male and female athletes

Advantages and disadvantages

👍 Minimal equipment – a stop watch and a mat.

👍 Quick and easy to perform.

👍 It can be carried out in most environments.

👎 Needs high levels of motivation to continue for one minute.

👎 It only assesses muscular endurance of the abdominal muscles. A person who has high levels of muscular endurance in their legs (such as a cyclist) may score poorly on this test.

Now try this

Phil is 20 years old and rows for his university rowing team.
He takes part in the one-minute sit-up test and completes 26 sit-ups.

1 State the component of fitness tested by the one-minute sit-up test.

2 Look at the table above and identify Phil's endurance rating for the one-minute sit-up test.

Flexibility

Flexibility is the range of motion available at the joints of the body. It includes a person's ability to move a joint fluidly through its complete range of movement.

Importance of flexibility?

The more **flexible** a person is, the more movement they have at their joints. Their muscle tissues and ligaments are more supple and longer than those of a less flexible person.

- Flexibility can be good in one area of a person's body but weak in another; for example, very flexible shoulders but less flexible hips.
- Flexibility can help to prevent injury. Flexible muscles can protect the body from injuries caused by overextension, such as when a football goalkeeper stretches their arms backwards to make a save.

Sports requiring flexibility

This component of fitness is used in all sports and activities. It allows the complete range of movement at the joints so that we can participate fully.

Sports where flexibility is ...	
a key component of performance	part of the overall profile
• Gymnastics	• Racket sports
• Diving	• Team sports

Sit and reach test

This fitness test measures the flexibility of the participant's hamstrings and lower back muscles. The length of their arms and legs should not affect how well they perform in this test.

 The participant sits with their legs straight and their feet against the board.

 Keeping their legs straight, they slowly reach as far forward as they possibly can, pushing the marker on the sit and reach board.

③ Record the measurement in centimetres of the furthest point reached.

④ Repeat the test three times and use the best result.

Equipment	Protocol
Sit and reach box.	Before taking part in the test, the participant should carry out an appropriate warm-up (see page 28 for routines). They should remove their shoes and wear clothing that does not restrict their movement.

Normative test data

Rating	Males (cm)	Females (cm)
Excellent	+17 to +27	+21 to +30
Good	+6 to +16	+ 11 to +20
Average	0 to +5	+1 to +10
Fair	–8 to –1	–7 to 0
Poor	–20 to –9	–15 to –8
Very poor	< –20	< –15

Normative data for males and females. The measuring scale for this test has the 0cm point at the level of the feet.

Advantages and disadvantages

👍 Minimal equipment is required – just a sit and reach box.

👍 The equipment is not expensive.

👍 The test is quick and easy to perform.

👍 It can be carried out in most environments.

👎 A person may be much more flexible in other areas of their body that are not tested in the sit and reach test.

👎 The reliability of the test results depends on how much time has been spent on the warm-up.

Now try this

Simon is male and Sara is female. They both achieve a result of +18 cm when they take the sit and reach test.

Using the table above, identify the flexibility rating for:

a Simon   **b** Sara.

Speed

Speed is how much time it takes a person to travel over a specified distance. Speed is essential in some sports and offers an advantage in many others.

Calculating speed

Use this equation to calculate speed:

$$\text{speed} = \frac{\text{distance covered}}{\text{time}}$$

In a 100m sprint race, the athlete must quickly get up from the blocks and start sprinting to reach their maximum speed as soon as possible.

Sports and activities that use speed

Sports where speed is ...	
a key component of performance	part of the overall profile
• Sprint events: 100m run, 25m swim, speed skating • Long jump	• Team sports: netball (to intercept the ball); basketball (dribbling with the ball) • Endurance events: 10k race when overtaking; cycle race for sprint finish

Thirty-metre sprint test

This fitness test measures how fast a person can run over a distance of 30m.

Equipment

Flat non-slip running surface, tape measure (or marked track), stop watch.

Protocol

The person taking the test should thoroughly warm up before taking the test (see page 28 for routines).

1. The participant starts behind the line in a stationary position.
2. Stand at the finishing line, and shout 'Go' as you start the stop watch.
3. The participant sprints as fast as they can over the 30m distance.
4. Stop the stop watch when they pass the line. Record the result in seconds, to the nearest tenth of a second.
5. The participant has a three-minute rest period and then repeats the test.
6. Use the best result from the two tests to compare with normative data tables.

Normative data

Rating	Males	Females
Excellent	<4.0s	<4.5s
Above average	4.2–4.0s	4.6–4.5s
Average	4.4–4.3s	4.8–4.7s
Below average	4.6–4.5s	5.0–4.9s
Poor	<4.6s	<5.0s

Source: Davis B et al.: *Physical Education and the Study of Sport*; 2000

Normative data for adult males and females. The results are given to the nearest tenth of a second.

Advantages and disadvantages

👍 This is a good test of speed for a person whose sport involves running in a straight line.

👍 The test does not require any expensive equipment.

👍 It is quick and easy to perform.

👎 The type or condition of the running surface can affect the results.

👎 The test only measures speed in a straight line and with no equipment. For example, in rugby a player has to dodge opponents and hold the ball when running at speed.

Now try this

The table gives the 30-metre sprint test times achieved by three different adult athletes.

1. Use the normative data table above to identify the speed rating that each athlete has achieved.

2. Explain whether you think the ratings achieved are what you would expect for athletes who practise these sports.

	Gender	Sport	Time (s)
a	Male	Triathlon	4.2
b	Female	100m sprint	3.7
c	Male	Shot put	5.2

Strength

Strength is the maximum force that can be generated by a muscle or muscle group. It is measured in kilograms (kg) or newtons (N).

Importance of strength

Strength is related to muscle mass:

- The larger a person's muscle mass, the more strength the person has. This is because muscle tissue produces force.
- The more muscle tissue a person has, the more force their muscles can produce.

Activities that use strength

Strength is needed in sports where the participant needs to move a heavy object or resist another person.

Sports where strength is ...	
a key component of performance	**part of the overall profile**
Moving heavy objects: • Weight lifting • Wrestling • Shot put	• Rugby (tackling, pushing against other players in the scrum) • Gymnastics

Hand grip dynamometer test

Measures strength of hand and forearm muscles.

Equipment

Hand grip dynamometer.

Protocol

1 Adjust the handle so that it fits the size of the hand of the person being tested.

2 The participant should hold the dynamometer in their dominant hand and allow their arm to hang by their side, with the dynamometer by their thigh.

3 The participant squeezes the dynamometer as hard as they can for around five seconds.

4 Record the reading (in kgw) from the dynamometer.

5 Repeat the test twice more, with at least a one-minute rest between tests. Record the results.

Males usually have more muscle mass than females, and muscle mass decreases with age so strength declines with age.

Normative test data

Rating	Females aged 15–19 years (kgw)
Excellent	>32
Good	28–31
Average	25–27
Below average	20–24
Poor	<20

Advantages and disadvantages

👍 Only the hand grip dynamometer is required.

👍 The test is quick and easy to perform.

👍 The test can be carried out in most places.

👎 The test only measures the strength of the forearms, which might not represent the strength of other muscle groups.

👎 The hand grip dynamometer can be expensive.

Now try this

Ola is a gymnast. Her rating in the hand grip dynamometer test was below average.

Explain whether this hand grip dynamometer test rating is a good indicator of Ola's overall body strength.

Do you think a gymnast might have high levels of strength in other areas of their body?

Power

Power is a combination of strength and speed. It is an important component of fitness in many sports.

Importance of power

In many sports, power is needed in order to apply the maximum force possible in the shortest time.

- On the starter's pistol, a sprinter pushes down on their starting blocks with as much power as they can, to push them up and out of the blocks to start sprinting as soon as possible.
- Power is also used in team sports where a player needs to be able to jump high (such as a basketball player jumping to perform a lay shot) or hit or kick an object with force (such as a football goalkeeper kicking the football down the pitch).

Activities that use power

- Power can also be applied to an object. A javelin thrower uses the power in their arm to throw the javelin as far as they can.

Sports where power is ...	
a key component of performance	**part of the overall profile**
• Boxing • Shot put • Power lifting	• Tennis (serving) • Sprinting (pushing off the starting blocks) • High jump (pushing off the ground)

Sargent jump test

The test measures the power in a person's legs. It is also known as the **vertical jump test**.

Equipment

Wall, chalk, ruler or tape measure.

Protocol

Before taking part in the test, the participant must be fully warmed up (see page 28 for routines).

1 The participant stands side on to the wall, with their feet flat on the floor.

2 With the hand closest to the wall, they reach as high as they can. Mark where their stretched fingers come to on the wall.

3 The participant then covers their fingers with chalk.

4 Again, standing side on to the wall, they crouch down and jump up as high as they can. At their highest point, the participant touches the wall to leave a chalk mark to show how high they have jumped.

5 Record the difference (in centimetres) between the participant's first mark and the chalk mark. This is the participant's score.

Normative test data

Rating	Males aged 16–19 years (cm)
Excellent	>65
Above average	50–65
Average	40–49
Below average	30–39
Poor	<30

Normative data tables are available for males and females of different ages. Males usually have a greater muscle mass than females so have more power. Power declines with age because muscle mass decreases as a person gets older.

Advantages and disadvantages

👍 The test assesses the power in a person's legs.

👍 It is quick and easy to perform.

👍 It does not require any expensive equipment.

👎 Jumping technique can affect the result. The participant must have a number of practice jumps to develop their technique.

👎 The test only measures the power in the legs and no muscles in the upper body.

Now try this

Jamie competes at a high level in the high jump. He scores an excellent rating in the vertical jump test. Gavin competes at a high level in the discus throwing event.

1 a Explain why the vertical jump test is a good measure of power for Jamie.

   b Explain why the vertical jump test is not a good measure of power for Gavin.

Body composition

Body composition is the proportion of fat mass and fat-free mass in the body. The fat-free mass is also called lean tissue, and consists of muscle, bone and vital organs.

What is body composition?

Our bodies are made up of the same parts – muscle, bone, organs, tissue, and fat. However, the percentage of body fat can vary immensely from person to person.

- The percentage of stored fat in a body versus the percentage of lean mass is the primary focus of body composition.
- Average amounts of body fat for females are around 25–31 per cent, and 18–24 per cent for males.

Relevance of body composition in sports

Sports where a particular body composition is beneficial	
Low body fat **Low muscle mass**	**High body fat** **High muscle mass**
• Jockey	• Sumo wrestler
Low body fat **High muscle mass**	**Mixed levels of body fat and muscle mass**
• Gymnast • Heavyweight boxer	• Racket sports • Team sports

Advantage of lower levels of body fat

Many athletes have lower percentages of body fat than the average because in some sports, higher amounts of body fat can have a negative effect on sporting performance.

Excess body fat increases body weight, which can make it more difficult to excel in sports such as long-distance running or high jump.

Assessing body composition

There are many ways of assessing body composition, some of which are used in gyms to help monitor body fat. This is useful for people who are trying to lose excess body fat.

Muscle tissue weighs more than body fat, so if a person has started to gain muscle mass from strength training, they might gain weight but still be losing body fat.

Having a low proportion of body fat helps high jumpers to be lighter so they are more able to lift high up from the ground and clear the bar.

Now try this

Sally takes part in 400 m hurdles. Her coach monitors her body composition and tells Sally that having high levels of body fat would have a negative effect on her performance.

Explain why having a high level of body fat would have a negative effect on hurdling performance.

When answering this question, think about what the athlete has to do when hurdling: run quickly around the track and jump hurdles.

Training for aerobic endurance

If you use the results of the Cooper 12-minute run test on page 2 to assess a person's level of aerobic endurance, you can choose appropriate training methods to improve it for their sport or activity.

Principles of aerobic training

Aerobic training aims to improve the efficiency of the cardiorespiratory system so that more oxygen and nutrients are delivered to the working muscles and more waste products are removed.

This allows the participant to take part in their sport for longer periods of time at the same intensity.

Types of training for developing aerobic endurance are:

1 interval training
2 continuous training
3 fartlek training.

Advantages and disadvantages

👍 Aerobic endurance training is good for all sports that last at least 30 minutes.

👍 No special facilities or equipment required, other than those for the participant's sport.

👍 It can take place inside or outside.

👎 If the training takes place outside, the weather can impact performance.

👎 You must have enough time for at least 30 minutes' regular training.

1 Interval training

Interval training involves exercising at 60–80 per cent Max HR followed by a recovery period.

- The time spent exercising can vary from a few seconds to many minutes.
- The recovery period may involve complete rest or exercising at very low intensity such as walking or jogging.
- To develop aerobic endurance, the length of the rest periods should be decreased and the exercise periods increased.

Advantages

👍 Interval training replicates a range of sports involving rest periods. For example, in netball, the players walk back to their positions after a team has scored before the game starts again.

2 Continuous training

Continuous training involves exercising at a constant intensity for at least 30 minutes. It can include jogging, swimming and cycling. The participant's heart rate (HR) should remain at 60–80% of their maximum. Revise intensity of training on page 17.

Advantages and disadvantages

👍 It is good for sports where a person exercises for long periods of time at the same intensity, such as a 10 km flat running race.

👎 It does not replicate the type of fitness needed for many sports, when the exercise intensity varies and the heart rate may go above 80% max.

👎 It can become tedious.

3 Fartlek training

Fartlek training combines continuous training with higher-intensity exercise.

- An example would be swimming at a set pace of 60–80 per cent maximum heart rate (Max HR) and then sprinting a few lengths beyond 80 per cent Max HR.
- Intensity can also be increased by using resistance, such as running uphill or with a weighted backpack.
- There are no rest periods in fartlek training.

Advantages and disadvantages

👍 Fartlek training helps to develop speed during the periods of higher-intensity training, as well as aerobic endurance during the periods of moderate-intensity training.

👍 This training method prepares participants for sports where they exercise at moderate intensity for long periods and then increase the intensity for brief periods. For example, in football, players jog continually up and down the pitch, and then occasionally do a fast sprint with the ball.

👎 Can be difficult to measure.

Now try this

Torin is a cross-country runner. He takes part in fartlek training and wants to increase the intensity of his training to help him prepare for a race.

Here you must give a reason for your answer.

Explain one method Torin can use to increase the intensity of his fartlek training.

Training for muscular endurance

Muscular endurance is usually needed in sports and activities where high levels of aerobic endurance are also required. Look back at muscular endurance and the one-minute sit-up test on page 3.

Principles of muscular endurance training

Muscular endurance training increases the ability of the trained muscles to contract repeatedly for long periods of time. Training for muscular endurance should include exercises:

- with a high number of repetitions (high reps)
- using low resistance or load (low weights).

Cycling is a good example of muscular endurance training for legs because it involves pushing down on the pedals many times (high reps) and the resistance is relatively low (low weights). Other methods of improving muscular endurance include circuit training and core stability training.

Circuit training

Circuit training involves stations of muscular endurance exercises arranged in a circuit. Participants carry out each exercise for a period of time before moving on to the next station. Short rest periods can be included between the stations.

Advantages and disadvantages

👍 It can be tailored to a specific sport, with drills from the sport included at some stations.

👍 Different muscle groups are exercised at each station to improve muscular endurance in the whole body.

👍 The stations can be changed at each training session to avoid boredom.

👍 Circuit training is usually a group exercise, which can help with motivation.

👎 Cards or signs for each station need to be made prior to the training.

👎 It takes time to set out the circuit with appropriate equipment.

Core stability training

Core stability is required for all sports and activities. It allows participants to maintain good posture and helps to prevent injuries to the back and neck.

There are many different types of core stability training methods, which concentrate on exercising the abdominals, obliques and muscles in the back. Examples include crunches, the plank, and leg raises.

Advantages and disadvantages

👍 No equipment is needed – most core stability exercises can be carried out using body weight alone.

👍 A stability ball can be used, which is inexpensive.

👍 It can be carried out at times that fit in with the participant's other commitments.

👎 High levels of motivation are needed to carry out exercises regularly.

👎 Exercises may need to be modified for the participant's level.

👎 A coach/instructor may be needed to advise on correct technique.

Now try this

Anita is taking part in circuit training for muscular endurance.

Describe how Anita should use weights in the circuit to develop her muscular endurance.

Think about the number of reps and what the load should be (how heavy the weights are).

Using a stability ball to perform sit-ups avoids having the hard floor surface underneath the spine. It helps to fully engage the core muscles as the participant has to balance on the ball while performing the sit-ups.

Training for flexibility

Flexibility training plays an important part in injury prevention and is beneficial for sporting performance. Sportspeople whose joints can move through their full range of movement are more able to perform specific sporting techniques correctly. Look back at the sit and reach test on page 4 which tests flexibility.

Methods of improving flexibility include static stretching, dynamic stretching and proprioceptive neuromuscular facilitation (PNF) stretching.

Static stretching

The participant gets into a position to target a specific muscle or muscle group, and holds the position to develop the stretch.

Static stretching can be done using your own body, another person or an object to keep the body part in the correct position. The stretch needs to be held for 12–30 seconds.

Advantages and disadvantages

👍 This helps to increase flexibility in specific areas of the body required for particular sports.

👍 As with all types of stretching, little or no equipment is needed, so there are no costs and no time required setting up equipment.

👎 High levels of motivation are needed to carry out exercises regularly.

👎 A coach/instructor may be needed to advise on correct technique.

Dynamic stretching

Dynamic stretching involves gradually increasing the range of movement of a muscle or group of muscles over a series of repetitions.

A dynamic stretch for the hamstrings

Advantages and disadvantages

👍 This helps to maintain an elevated heart rate, so it is good to include in a warm-up to help get the body ready for training.

👍 No equipment is needed so there are no costs and no time required setting up equipment.

👎 If a participant is not sufficiently warmed up, dynamic stretching could cause injury as they might overstretch when carrying out the movement.

Proprioceptive neuromuscular facilitation (PNF) stretching

PNF stretching requires a partner to provide resistance.

1 The participant stretches the muscle or muscle group as far as possible.

2 The partner holds the body part being stretched while the participant pushes against their partner for 6–10 seconds.

3 The participant then relaxes the muscle while the partner pushes the body part to increase the stretch.

The process is repeated about three times.

Advantages and disadvantages

👍 It helps to develop flexibility at a faster rate than other types of flexibility training.

👎 Another person is needed and so the stretches cannot be performed alone.

👎 There is a risk of injury if the stretching partner lacks experience.

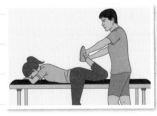

A PNF stretch for the quadriceps

Now try this

PNF is a type of flexibility training.

1 Identify two other types of flexibility training.

2 State one reason why a person might choose PNF training rather than other types of flexibility training.

For question 2, choose an advantage of PNF stretching that isn't a feature of the other types.

Training for speed

Speed is important for athletic track events and sprint cycling, as well as for team games (for example, when sprinting to intercept the ball or get ahead of an opponent). You can revise speed and the 30-metre sprint test on page 5.

The range of training methods designed to develop speed includes sprint training, sport-specific speed training (speed, agility and quickness – SAQ) and interval training.

Sprint training

Sprint training involves completing a set distance as fast as possible, such as in running, cycling or swimming.

- Resistance can be used to increase the load the participant has to sprint against. This overloads the muscles to make them stronger.
- Assisted sprinting, such as running downhill, makes sprinting easier and helps the muscles to get used to the process of moving at speed.

Resistance can be provided by using bungee ropes, a parachute or sprinting uphill.

Advantages and disadvantages

👍 It is good for sports that involve travelling at speed.

👍 It is good for sports that require sprinting in a straight line.

👍 Equipment can be used to add resistance and variety.

👎 The equipment can be expensive.

👎 It is only useful for sports that involve sprinting in one direction.

Sport-specific speed training (SAQ)

For this type of speed training, SAQ equipment and training principles are used.

This method involves sprinting and then changing direction over a set course which is designed to replicate sport-specific speed requirements.

SAQ involves sport-specific drills such as running around or over obstacles.

Advantages and disadvantages

👍 It can be made sport-specific.

👍 It is good for sports that include changes of direction when sprinting.

👍 The equipment is cheap and easy to use.

👍 The equipment adds variety and helps prevent boredom.

👎 Time is needed to set up the equipment prior to the training.

Interval training

For interval training that aims to develop speed, very short, high-intensity work periods are followed by a rest or recovery period.

Advantages and disadvantages

👍 It is good for sports that have varied intensity with recovery periods.

👍 No equipment is needed.

👍 No training facility is required.

👎 It does not always replicate sport-specific movements.

Now try this

Freddie is a rugby player. He wants to improve his speed to help his rugby-playing performance.

Choose one method of speed training and give a reason why this method is suitable for improving speed for Freddie's sport.

Training for strength

The purpose of strength training is to increase the size of a person's muscles. The larger the muscles, the more force they can exert and the more strength they have. Look back at page 6 to revise strength and the hand grip dynamometer.

Principles of strength training

To increase strength, muscle tissue needs to be overloaded using heavy weights to cause muscle **hypertrophy** (an increase in muscle size). Strength training exercises involve carrying out low numbers of reps using heavy weights. Free weights and resistance machines can be used to help increase muscle size and improve a person's strength.

Free weights

A free weight is one that is not attached to machinery.

- A dumbbell is a short bar with a weight at each end, used with one in each hand.
- A barbell is a longer bar with a weight at each end, used with both hands.

Dumbbells are available in different weights to suit different levels of strength and to allow for progression.

Advantages

👍 Free weight training increases strength over a large range of movements.

👍 They allow the participant to focus on certain movements or specific muscle groups.

👍 Targeting specific muscle groups helps increase strength for particular sports.

👍 Free weights can be stored and used at home.

👍 The same equipment can be used to train different muscle groups.

Disadvantages

👎 Weight training exercises rarely replicate the movements carried out in sport fully – although muscle size will increase, the range of movement actually used in sport might not.

👎 Training cannot be carried out alone – a spotter is needed to ensure the participant's safety.

👎 To ensure the participant's safety, training should not be carried out when fatigued. This can increase the chance of not being able to lift the weight and incurring injuries.

Resistance machines

Resistance machines use stacks of weights attached to pulleys or air pressure to provide resistance.

Each machine is designed to perform one type of strength training exercise, and so only permits specific movement patterns to train specific muscles or groups of muscles.

Advantages and disadvantages

👍 They can increase the strength of targeted muscles and muscle groups for particular sports.

👍 They are safer than free weights for people new to weight training – there is less chance of injury from not being able to lift the weight.

👍 Participants can train alone.

👎 The equipment is expensive.

👎 You might need to join a gym or leisure centre to use the equipment.

👎 Each machine usually exercises only one muscle or muscle group, so many different pieces of equipment are required.

Now try this

Molly wants to improve her strength but has never carried out any strength training before.

Explain which method of strength training you would recommend for Molly.

Think about the two types of equipment used for strength training. Which one is easiest and safest for a person who is new to strength training? Make sure you give the reason for your choice.

Training for power

Power training involves using lower weights or resistance than strength training, and the types of exercises carried out allow the participant to perform a high number of repetitions. This simulates repeated use of power in sports such as the shot put, basketball and gymnastics. Look back to page 7 to revise power and the Sargent jump test. Plyometrics, anaerobic hill sprints and CrossFit are all training methods for improving power.

Plyometrics

Plyometric training involves making a muscle produce its maximum force in the fastest possible time.

- It uses movements which lengthen the muscle and then immediately shorten it, such as jumping on and off benches or over bars to develop power in the legs.
- The shorter the time between the lengthening and shortening of the muscle, the more power is generated.

Advantages and disadvantages

👍 It can be targeted for the muscle groups that require power.

👍 The equipment usually consists of benches or boxes, which are cheap and relatively easy to set up.

👍 It can be performed alone at times to suit the individual.

👎 Benches and bars need to be set up.

👎 It can cause injury as the muscles have to withstand high levels of stress.

Upper body plyometric training – the participant does a press-up then pushes hard off the ground to lift their upper body into the air before landing back into a press-up.

Anaerobic hill training

This training involves repeatedly running up a hill as fast as possible. The participant then has a recovery period walking back down the hill.

- The steepness of the hill has an impact on the intensity a person works at for this type of training, so participants should try to find a hill at the right incline for them.
- This type of training is anaerobic as the systems used to provide energy for it do not require oxygen.

Advantages and disadvantages

👍 It is beneficial for sports that are carried out at high intensity and involve running.

👍 No setting up or costs involved.

👍 It can be performed alone at convenient times.

👎 It is only suitable for sports that involve running.

👎 Access to a hill is needed.

👎 It is a high-intensity training method, which is not appropriate for people with low levels of fitness.

CrossFit

This type of training involves a variety of exercises including:

- using body weight as a form of resistance
- lifting weights
- aerobic-based exercises.

A range of different equipment can be used to add variety and interest to the training.

Advantages and disadvantages

👍 It can target specific areas of the body.

👍 The equipment is relatively cheap and does not take long to set up.

👍 Intensity can be varied to cater for different ability levels.

👎 You need to attend a class because there is a wide range of exercises, which require specialist knowledge.

Now try this

Cathy is a basketball player. She takes part in plyometric training to improve her power for basketball.

Give **two** advantages for Cathy of taking part in plyometric training to improve her basketball performance.

The FITT principles

The letters of FITT stand for the key principles to follow when planning a training programme. These are **Frequency, Intensity, Type,** and **Time**. The FITT principles should be used when planning weekly training programmes to improve targeted components of fitness. Participants at all levels, from complete beginners to elite athletes, should follow these principles to ensure that their training programme will be effective.

Frequency – How many training sessions per week?

Intensity – How hard will the participant train? (for example, as a percentage of maximum heart rate)

The four FITT principles

Type – What type of training method and exercises will be used?

Time – How long will the training session last?

Revise each of the FITT principles in more detail on pages 16–19.

🌐 Real world Applying the FITT principles

This an example of a training programme where the FITT principles have been applied.

Day	Training
Mon	30 minutes continuous training Jogging – 60% Max HR
Tues	Rest day
Wed	30 minutes continuous training Jogging – 60% Max HR
Thu	Rest day
Fri	30 minutes continuous training Jogging – 60% Max HR
Sat	60 minutes continuous training Cycling – 60% Max HR
Sun	60 minutes flexibility training (static stretching) Yoga class – moderate intensity

Frequency has been applied – there are five training sessions this week.

Intensity for jogging and cycling is given as percentage of Max HR. The intensity for flexibility training is based on a scale of low/moderate/high intensity.

Type of training is given (continuous, flexibility) along with type of exercise (jogging, cycling, static stretching).

Time is given – each training session lasts between 30 and 60 minutes.

Make sure that the **type** of exercise chosen will help the participant achieve their goals. Yoga is a popular activity for developing flexibility.

Now try this

The FITT principles are used to plan training programmes.

1 Identify what the letters F and I stand for in the FITT principles.

2 Give an example of how you can apply each of these principles in a weekly training programme.

Frequency

In the FITT principles, frequency means the number of training sessions completed every week.

Deciding frequency

When deciding on the frequency of training sessions you need to strike a balance between:

- providing sufficient stress for adaptations in the body to occur
- allowing enough rest periods for the body to heal and repair from the exercise sessions.

Progression and overload

You must take progression and overload into account when planning the frequency of sessions in a training programme.

There should be a gradual increase in stress placed upon the body, combined with a gradual increase in the frequency of training sessions.

Revise progressive overload on page 21.

 Beginner's training programme

Beginners should start with about three training sessions per week, and build up to more sessions per week as their bodies adapt to the training.

Week	1	2	3	4	5	6
Frequency of training sessions	3	3	4	4	4	5

This training programme provides a gradual increase in the number of training sessions each week.

Why increase the frequency of training sessions?

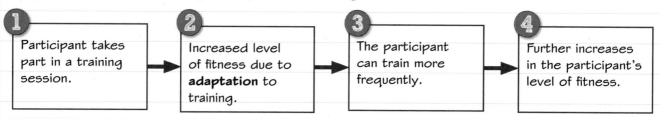

1 Participant takes part in a training session. → **2** Increased level of fitness due to **adaptation** to training. → **3** The participant can train more frequently. → **4** Further increases in the participant's level of fitness.

Adaptations are the body's responses to training that make it more able to cope with the stresses of the exercise. For example, muscle tissue adapts to strength training by getting bigger.

Frequency for training specific components of fitness

- **Muscular strength/muscular endurance** – two to three sessions per week.
- **Flexibility** – should be incorporated into the warm-up and cool down of every exercise session.
- **Speed and power** – frequency will depend on the specific sport, but two to three sessions a week are usually appropriate.
- **Aerobic endurance** – the weekly training programme should include a minimum of three sessions that target aerobic endurance, such as fartlek training.

Running up sand dunes and jogging back down is an example of fartlek training.

Now try this

Adam is training for a 10 km road race.

1. Identify the minimum number of weekly training sessions Adam should complete to improve his aerobic endurance.

Jess is a 400 m hurdler and trains four times a week.

2. Identify how many times Jess should take part in flexibility training.

Intensity

In the FITT principles, intensity means how hard a person is exercising or how much effort they are putting into the exercise. It is important to exercise at the right intensity so that the training targets the right component of fitness and leads to adaptations.

Deciding intensity

As with frequency, the intensity of the activity must overload the body so it will adapt. But the intensity must not be so high that it causes overtraining. Revise overtraining on page 22.

The level of intensity can be altered by changing factors in the training session such as:

- increasing or decreasing the weight used (resistance) in strength training
- covering a longer or shorter distance in aerobic endurance training
- spending more or less time exercising.

Measuring intensity

The intensity of training can be measured using one of these two methods.

 The Borg Scale – Rate of perceived exertion (RPE)

The Borg RPE scale ranges from 6 (rest) to 20 (exhaustion). The person exercising indicates the number that represents how hard they are working.

Score	Perceived exertion
6	No exertion
7–8	Extremely light
9–10	Very light
11–12	Light
13–14	Somewhat hard
15–16	Hard
17–18	Very hard
19	Extremely hard
20	Maximum exertion

Multiply the score by 10 to get an estimate of the person's heart rate (in beats per minute) during the workout: RPE × 10 = HR (bpm)

2 **Percentage of maximum heart rate (Max HR)**

For some types of activity, working at the right intensity means a person exercising so that their heart is beating at a percentage of their Max HR.

Use the formula: Max HR = 220 – age

Measuring HR

Pulse points: you can measure HR at pulse points. The radial pulse on the wrist and the carotid pulse in the neck are good places to measure HR. Count the number of heart beats for 30 seconds, and multiply by 2.

Technology: there are lots of technological devices that can be used to measure HR, including smart watches, apps and HR monitors.

This chest strap monitors heart rate and the wrist watch records the information.

 For example: Zoya is 15 years old. She wants to work at 70 per cent of her Max HR to train her aerobic endurance.

Step 1 Calculate Zoya's Max HR:

Max HR = 220 – 15 = 205 bpm

Step 2 Then work out 70 per cent of her Max HR:

205 × 70/100 = 144 bpm

Now try this

Susie is 18 years old and takes part in continuous training. She wants to ensure that she is working at an intensity of 70–80 per cent Max HR, in order to train aerobic endurance.

1 Calculate Susie's Max HR.

2 Calculate 70 per cent of her Max HR.

3 Calculate 80 per cent of her Max HR.

- Give your answers as the number of beats per minute (bpm).

- If your answer has any decimal places, round to the nearest whole number.

Type

Make sure that the type of training you choose targets a specific component of fitness. You will need to consider both the type of exercise the person will take part in and the training method.

Which training type?

The type of training selected for a training programme should be determined by:

- the sport or activity the person takes part in
- the component of fitness the person wants to develop.

 Specific training

A shot-put thrower wants to improve their strength. An appropriate activity would be free weight training, targeting the main muscles used to throw the shot put.

Selecting the type of exercise and training method

Component of fitness	Types of exercise (examples)	Training methods (examples)
Aerobic endurance	Running, cycling, swimming, rowing	Continuous training, fartlek training, interval training
Muscular endurance	Body weight exercises – tricep dips, press-ups, lunges, squats, sit-ups	Circuit training
Strength	Free weights – bicep curls, bench press, knee extensions, hamstring curls, shoulder press	Resistance machines, free weights
Flexibility	Standing stretches, lying down stretches, using a partner or object to stretch	Static stretching, dynamic stretching, PNF stretching
Power	Bounding, hopping, sprinting up a hill, using different types of equipment to develop power in upper and lower body	Plyometrics, anaerobic hill sprints, CrossFit
Speed	Sprinting on a running track, using sport-specific speed and agility equipment	Interval training, sprint training, SAQ

Variety of training methods

It is important to vary the training methods to avoid boredom.

 A person who wants to develop their aerobic endurance so that they can run 5km should carry out running-specific training, but use different types of training in different environments. Appropriate training activities could include:

- running on a treadmill
- cross-country running
- running round an athletics track
- running with a group of people in a running club
- using a cross trainer.

Running with a group can help to prevent boredom. Park Runs are free and staffed by volunteers – they cover a distance of 5km and are held weekly in many towns and cities across the country.

Now try this

Tanya is a gymnast. She wants to improve her power so that she can jump higher when performing her floor routine.

You can revise the different training methods for developing power on page 14.

1. Identify a training method that Tanya could use to improve her power.
2. Describe a type of exercise that Tanya could carry out to improve her power.

Time

The length of time spent in a training session should be enough to encourage progressive overload. It should also be appropriate to the type of training and the component of fitness being trained.

High-intensity training (HIT), cardiovascular and fat-burning activities

How long you should spend in a training session for these activities will depend on the component of fitness being developed and the purpose of the training.

- HIT for developing aerobic and anaerobic fitness – short duration (30 seconds to 1 minute), with rest periods no longer than 30 seconds. Training sessions usually last up to 30 minutes.
- Cardiovascular activities for developing aerobic endurance – at least 20 minutes.
- Fat-burning activities use body fat as a fuel so are good for people who want to lose excess body fat – at least 28 minutes.

You can revise the different training zones on page 25.

Strength and muscular endurance activities

Strength and endurance training timeframes are based on the number of sets and reps for each muscle group. The participant must train for the time it takes to complete the required number of sets.

- The number of reps is how many times the exercise is repeated.
- The number of sets is how many lots of reps the participant completes.

For example, to develop muscular endurance of the biceps, the training could be: bicep curls – three sets of 15 reps.

Strength training requires a:
- low number of sets
- low number of reps
- high load/heavy weights.

Muscular endurance training requires a:
- high number of sets
- high number of reps
- low load/light weights.

Now try this

Sean is 28 years old, and is trying to lose excess body fat.

1 Identify one type of exercise Sean could take part in to help him lose body fat.

2 State the minimum length of time Sean should take part in the exercise, in order to lose excess body fat.

- Select exercises that Sean can keep performing for at least the minimum amount of time.
- Activities that are used to develop aerobic endurance or muscular endurance will be appropriate here.

Principles of training: specificity

As well as the FITT principles, there are six further principles of training that you can use to plan a training programme. Using these principles will help improve a participant's physical fitness and sporting performance.

Training zones
Working at the correct intensity
Revise this on page 25

Participant differences and needs
Taking into account current levels of fitness and sport
Revise this on page 24

Specificity
Training for specific components of fitness
Revise this below

The principles of training

Reversibility
Effects of stopping training
Revise this on page 23

Overtraining
Risks of increasing workload too quickly
Revise this on page 22

Progressive overload
Gradually increasing workload
Revise this on page 21

What is specificity?

Specificity means choosing a training method that develops a specific component of fitness which benefits participation in a particular sport or activity.

The remaining five principles of training can then be applied to this specific training method.

Applying the principle of specificity

To apply the principle of specificity, you need to make sure that the training methods are matched to the demands of the sport or activity that the participant is training for. For example:

- A netball player could take part in circuit training to develop muscular endurance. The stations would focus on upper body and lower body muscular endurance, as the arms and legs are used to play netball. Some circuit stations could include netball-specific drills such as passing and dodging.
- A long-distance cyclist could take part in road cycling to develop aerobic endurance. They could also train at home on their bike using a turbo trainer, use a stationary bike in a gym and take part in spin classes.

A turbo trainer is a device for cycling training. It allows you to pedal a normal bicycle but without travelling anywhere.

Now try this

Ryan is a rower. He is going to take part in a race in six weeks' time, and wants to improve his fitness for the event.

Describe **two** ways in which Ryan could use the principle of specificity to improve his rowing performance.

Progressive overload

Progressive overload means gradually increasing the participant's workload over time.

Applying the principle of progressive overload

Fitness can only be improved by **overloading** – training at a higher level than you normally do. Working harder in exercise sessions stimulates your body to adapt to the training. This will improve your fitness levels in the component of fitness being trained.

- If you do not overload, your fitness will not improve beyond its current levels.
- Overload is achieved by increasing the frequency, intensity and/or length of time spent training.
- Overloading should be **progressive** – the training programme should provide a gradual increase in the frequency, intensity or time spent exercising. This is necessary to avoid injury and overtraining.

Revise overtraining on page 22.

Progressive overload using time

A person who is training to take part in a long-distance race might undertake continuous training to improve their aerobic endurance.

- To apply progressive overload in this situation, gradually increase the **time** the participant spends training.
- As the length of the training sessions increases, the distance the participant runs will naturally also increase over the course of the training programme.
- For example, they can run further in a 50-minute session than in a 30-minute session.

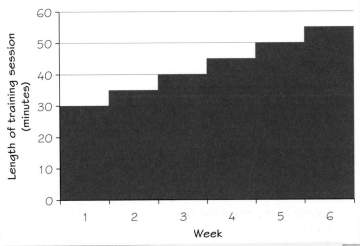

Start with a short training time and gradually increase.

Progressive overload using percentage of maximum heart rate (Max HR)

You can apply progressive overload to a training programme by increasing the **intensity** at which the participant exercises, using percentage of Max HR.

- In interval training, the training sessions could be planned, so that each week the percentage of the participant's Max HR is increased to a slightly higher level during exercise periods.
- Once the desired maximum intensity has been achieved, increase the time spent exercising at the higher intensity in order to maintain progressive overload.

Progressive overload in strength training

To train for **strength**, the weights or resistance used should progressively increase. The participant's muscles will continually have to adapt to meet the demands of lifting increasingly heavier weights.

Week 1   Week 2   Week 3   Week 4   Week 5   Week 6

The overload can be achieved by keeping the number of reps and sets the same, but increasing the weight lifted.

Now try this

Give a definition of progressive overload.

Overtraining

Overtraining occurs when the training workload is increased too quickly. There is a greater risk of injury or of fitness levels not improving due to fatigue.

The effects of overtraining

If a person takes on too much training too soon, or does not have sufficient rest periods after training, they are at risk of overtraining.

- When someone is overtraining, their body is not able to recover sufficiently between training sessions and is in a weakened state, so it is more likely to become injured.

- Overtraining also results in no adaptation to training taking place, so the person does not have any fitness gains from their training sessions.

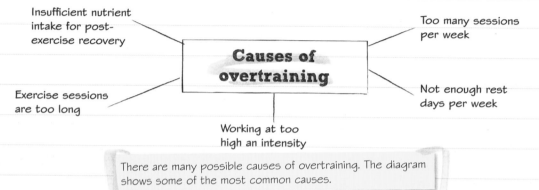

Insufficient nutrient intake for post-exercise recovery

Too many sessions per week

Causes of overtraining

Exercise sessions are too long

Not enough rest days per week

Working at too high an intensity

There are many possible causes of overtraining. The diagram shows some of the most common causes.

Applying the principle of overtraining

To prevent overtraining, every training programme should have a rest day where no training is carried out.

Appropriate nutrition is also important, such as:

- consuming enough protein-based foods to help with muscle repair

- consuming enough carbohydrates to replenish the body's energy stores.

A rest day is essential in any training programme. This allows the body time to recover and for adaptations to occur in response to the training sessions already completed.

Having a nutritious diet plays an important role in preventing overtraining. Revise nutrition for sport and activity on pages 31–42.

Now try this

Yang has been taking part in interval training over a six-week period. He has continually increased the time he spends training and the intensity of his workload, but recently he has noticed that his fitness levels are not improving.

Explain one reason why Yang's fitness levels are not improving.

Reversibility

Reversibility means that the fitness gains that have been made from previous training start to decline, and a person starts to lose their fitness levels. Reversibility can be summed up by the term, 'Use it or lose it'.

Why does reversibility happen?

Reversibility occurs when a person is not able to take part in training for a period of time. This could be due to illness, injury or other factors such as going on holiday and not having access to training facilities.

Injury is one of the main reasons that reversibility occurs.

The effects of reversibility on fitness

Reversibility is also known as **detraining**. When a person doesn't take part in training for some time, any training adaptations that have been developed as a result of the training will deteriorate.

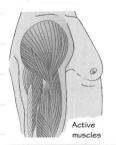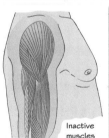

Active muscles   Inactive muscles

The trained muscle on the left is much larger than the untrained muscle on the right.

Adaptation

An adaptation is a response of the body to training that makes it more able to withstand the stresses of the training. Types of adaptation include:

✓ an increase in muscle size from strength training.

✓ an increase in capillaries around muscle tissue from muscular endurance training.

These adaptations allow a participant to improve in the component of fitness that is being trained.

However, these improvements are reversible. If training stops, the body will eventually return to its pre-exercise state.

✓ This could mean reduced muscle size or a reduced number of capillaries around muscle tissue.

Applying the principle of reversibility

A person who has had a period away from training, for whatever reason, will need to work out how this has affected their fitness levels.

- Taking part in fitness tests and comparing their results to previous fitness test results is a good way of doing this.
- They will then need to restart their training programme at a level appropriate to their current, somewhat reduced fitness levels.

Now try this

Identify one reason why an athlete might experience reversibility.

Differences and needs

A successful training programme will meet a participant's individual needs. These needs include:

- choosing a component of fitness that needs to be trained based on fitness test data
- relating the chosen fitness training method(s) to their sport or activity.

Applying the principle of participant differences and needs

Follow these steps to ensure that training meets the participant's individual needs.

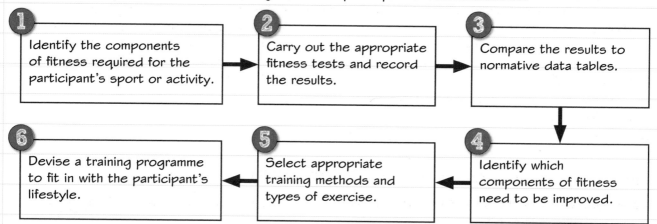

1 Identify the components of fitness required for the participant's sport or activity.

2 Carry out the appropriate fitness tests and record the results.

3 Compare the results to normative data tables.

6 Devise a training programme to fit in with the participant's lifestyle.

5 Select appropriate training methods and types of exercise.

4 Identify which components of fitness need to be improved.

Training methods

The training methods selected must be appropriate to train the identified components of fitness.

The types of exercise used for each training method should be sport-specific.

Revise the principle of specificity on page 20.

Individual lifestyle

It is important that the training is accessible to the individual. They must be able to:

- get to the location of the training
- afford to take part in the training
- fit the training around other commitments such as homework, work or family.

Meeting an individual's needs

To meet the participant's needs, the training programme should be:

- appropriate for their sport or activity
- appropriate for their fitness levels
- chosen to suit their likes and dislikes
- accessible – the equipment and facilities must be available and affordable
- varied, to avoid boredom and to train a range of body areas and/or components of fitness.

On page 26, you can revise gathering information to devise a personalised training programme.

The cost of taking part in training might include the cost of any special clothing, footwear and equipment required, as well as the hire of facilities, gym membership or class fees.

Now try this

Jardine takes part in the 100m sprint race.

1 Identify **two** components of fitness that are used to perform the 100 m sprint.
2 Explain **one** method of fitness training that would meet Jardine's individual needs.

Training zones

A training zone is the correct intensity at which a person should exercise in order to experience fitness improvement.

Why are training zones used?

To improve particular components of fitness, the participant must work at a specific training intensity. For example, to train for aerobic fitness, an individual must work at a lower intensity than someone who wants to train for anaerobic fitness.

- Working above or below the specified training zone will result in the incorrect component of fitness being trained.
- If the training zone is at too low a level, there will be no training effect.

Revise the FITT principle of intensity on page 17.

Anaerobic fitness

- Anaerobic fitness is required for sports that don't use oxygen as the main supply of energy, such as the 100 m sprint.
- Anaerobic fitness training is only recommended for people who already have good levels of fitness, as it can be harmful to the health of someone with low levels of fitness.

Percentage of maximum heart rate (Max HR) and training zones

A percentage of Max HR is used to calculate how hard you should work your heart to develop either aerobic or anaerobic fitness.

Warm-up or cool down zone		50–60% of Max HR	This zone can also be used for people new to training and to maintain current fitness levels.
Fat-burning zone		60–70% of Max HR	In this zone, body fat is used to provide energy. It is good for people who wish to lose excess body fat.
Aerobic training zone		70–80% of Max HR	This zone is used to develop aerobic endurance.
Anaerobic training zone		80–100% of Max HR	In this zone, the anaerobic energy systems are used to produce energy.

Calculating heart rates for the training zones

Max HR = 220 – age

50% Max HR = 50/100 × Max HR

60% Max HR = 60/100 × Max HR

70% Max HR = 70/100 × Max HR

80% Max HR = 80/100 × Max HR

100% Max HR = Max HR

Revise methods of measuring and estimating heart rate on page 17.

Now try this

1 Sunita is 22 years old. Calculate her maximum heart rate.

2 Calculate what Sunita's minimum and maximum heart rate should be for training in the aerobic training zone.

Remember to give your answers in beats per minute (bpm) and round your answers to the nearest whole number.

Fitness programme: gathering information

A fitness programme should be appropriate for the person who will be using it. You need to know the essential information that a fitness programme should include, and how to tailor the programme for the needs of the individual.

6 Components of a session plan

5 Safe design

Information needed for a fitness programme

4 Appropriate components of fitness

3 Objectives

1 Personal information

2 Aims

Using a person-centred approach

Using a person-centred approach means finding out more about the participant and using their personal information to help design the training programme. Personal information you need to gather includes:

- the participant's current state of health
- the activities they like and dislike
- their availability for exercise.

Using questionnaires to gather personal information

A **PAR-Q** is a type of health-screening questionnaire used to assess a person's medical history.

- It is designed to discover any risk factors that may make physical activity inadvisable.
- All the questions have yes/no answer choices. If the person answers yes to any question, they should consult a doctor before taking part in physical activity.

A **lifestyle questionnaire** is used to gain an overview of how the participant's lifestyle might impact on the design of a fitness programme.

A lifestyle questionnaire should include questions on:

- current activity levels
- drinking alcohol
- stress levels
- diet
- smoking
- sleep.

If you answer yes, to any questions, please give details below.

Question	Yes	No
1 Has your doctor ever told you that you have a heart condition?	☐	☐

Example of a question on a health-screening questionnaire

Confidentiality

Any information you take from a participant must be kept confidential, in line with the latest Data Protection Act. This means that the information should be stored securely so that no unauthorised person can gain access to it.

Setting aims and objectives

The overall **aim** of a fitness programme is what the participant hopes to be able to achieve. Some common aims are to:

- improve sporting performance
- lose excess body fat
- be fit enough to take part in an endurance event
- build muscle or to increase strength.

Objectives are all the things the participant needs to do in order to achieve their main aim; for example:

- Take part in four swimming training sessions per week, two of which will be in open water.

Now try this

Explain why a PAR-Q should be completed before a participant takes part in sport or physical activity.

Remember that PAR-Q stands for pre-activity readiness questionnaire.

Programme design

The information you have gathered from the participant (revised on page 26) will help you to build a fitness programme to help them achieve their fitness aims and objectives.

Choosing appropriate components of fitness

The training programme should target one or more of the components of fitness:

- aerobic endurance
- muscular endurance
- flexibility
- speed
- strength
- power.

The components of fitness that are important for the participant will be determined by their sport or activity and the participant's main aim (revised on page 26).

- Results from fitness tests will highlight which components of fitness need to be improved.
- It is also important to incorporate training to maintain high levels of fitness in components where the participant is already strong.

Revise the components of fitness and fitness tests on pages 2–7.

Fitness programme design

When designing the fitness programme, you need to include:

- times to exercise
- types of training and exercises.

Revise training methods for each component of fitness on pages 9–14.

Where possible, try to find ways to incorporate fitness training into the participant's everyday lifestyle:

- A participant who works close to a gym could take part in training sessions during their lunch hour.
- If a participant lives close to work, some of the exercise sessions could involve running or cycling to work.

Safe design

To make sure that the fitness programme is safe for the participant, the exercises must be at the right level for their current fitness. This will include:

- setting exercises at the right level of intensity
- selecting appropriate training methods.

For example, it might be safer for a person who is new to weight training to use fixed resistance machines rather than free weights, as there is less chance of injury from performing the lift incorrectly or dropping the weight.

To avoid injury, make sure the participant knows how to carry out each training method correctly.

Involving the participant

It is vital that the participant is involved in the programme design. You should consult the participant on:

- setting the aims and objectives – this will motivate the participant to take part in and persevere with the fitness programme
- deciding which days they will train on and for how long – based on their availability
- selecting the types of exercises – to ensure that they are enjoyable.

Now try this

Alex plays for a club rugby team. His fitness test results show that he needs to improve his strength.

1. State **one** training method that could be included in Alex's fitness programme to improve his strength.

2. Explain **two** ways in which Alex's coach can ensure that the fitness programme is safe for Alex to use.

Warm-up

Every training session in a fitness programme should have three components: a warm-up, the main activity or activities, and a cool down. You will need to be able to plan appropriate activities for each of these components.

Why warm up?

A warm-up is important to prepare the body for exercise. It increases:

- heart and breathing rates
- the temperature of the muscles
- the range of movement available at the joints and muscles.

There are three components to a warm-up: pulse raiser, mobiliser and stretch.

Avoiding injury

If you don't warm up properly before taking part in exercise, the muscles and ligaments will not be warm enough to allow them to stretch to the degree needed to perform sport or physical activity.

This puts you at greater risk of picking up injuries such as a muscle strain or a ligament sprain.

① Pulse raiser

This is the first part of a warm-up. The pulse raiser increases blood flow around the body:

- The contracting of the muscles during the pulse raiser generates heat, which warms up the blood.
- This increases the temperature of the body.

There should be a progressive increase in the intensity of pulse raiser activities, for example from a brisk walk to a slow jog then to a faster jog. Games that gradually increase pulse rate can also be included in the pulse raiser.

② Mobiliser

The second part of the warm-up mobilises the joints of the body, ready for participation in sport and physical activity.

This process increases the production of synovial fluid in the joints:

- This helps the bones that meet at the joint to slide over each other more easily, and increases the range of movement available at the joint.

The main joints of the body include the knees, hips, shoulders, ankles and wrists.

③ Stretch

The main muscles that are going to be used in the sport or physical activity should be stretched during the last part of the warm-up. Static stretches and dynamic stretches can be used:

- **Static stretches** – there is no movement, while the person holds the stretch for a short period of time.
- **Dynamic stretches** – these are active movements that stretch the muscles but the position is not held.

Revise static and dynamic stretches on page 11.

Duration of warm-up

Around 5–10 minutes is usually enough for the warm-up, but the exact duration will depend on a variety of factors.

In cold conditions, more time will be needed for the warm-up, as it will take longer to increase the temperature of the body.

People who are new to exercising will need longer, as more time is needed to:

- teach the correct techniques for each part of the warm-up
- ensure that the participant carries out the movements safely and in a controlled manner.

Now try this

Name **two** components of a warm-up.

A component is a section of the warm-up. A warm-up has three components, but you only need to include two in your answer here.

Main activities

The main activity or activities will be the longest component of each session in a fitness programme. During this part of the session, the participant will be working at the highest intensity.

Main activities to improve specific components of fitness

It is very important to select activities that will help the participant meet their main fitness goal. The table shows examples of main activities for different sports and fitness goals.

Sport or activity	Fitness goal	Type of activity
Tennis	Improve speed	Sprint training and SAQ
Gymnastics	Improve power	Plyometrics and CrossFit
10 km cross-country run	Improve aerobic endurance	Continuous training
Netball	Improve muscular endurance	Circuit training with netball drills

Revise the types of activity for training each component of fitness on pages 9–14 and 18.

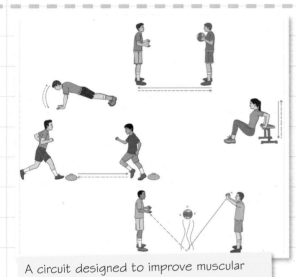

A circuit designed to improve muscular endurance for netball

Duration of main activities

The main activities will usually last:
- 15–20 minutes in a half-hour session
- around 45 minutes in a 1-hour session.

If training for a specific component of fitness, the duration of the main activity must meet the requirements for that type of training:
- Continuous training should be carried out for at least 20 minutes.
- Fat-burning activities should last for at least 28 minutes.
- Interval training and circuit training require rest periods.
- Continuous training involves continuous exercise, without a break.

Main activities to improve sporting technique

The main component in some exercise sessions could focus on improving the participant's sporting techniques. Types of activities might include the following:

Adapted games

The rules of the game are changed in order to practise the targeted skills or techniques.

Sport-specific drills

The drills for the targeted skill gradually increase in demand during the session:

- Isolated practice – practising the skill on its own, such as chest-passing the ball to a partner
- Travel – practising the skill with travel, such as chest-passing then running and stopping in time to receive a pass
- Unopposed drills – practising the skill in a small group, using travel but no opposition
- Opposed drills – practising while the opposition try to get the ball
- Pressurised drills – pressure is added, such as timing, speed or more attackers than defenders.

Now try this

1 Identify the minimum amount of time for the main part of a training session involving continuous training.
2 Identify two types of activity that could be included during the main activity to develop a person's sporting technique.

Cool down

The final component in any fitness programme is cooling down. You must remember to include a cool down activity that is appropriate for the type of activity that the participant has done.

Why cool down?

1 Cooling down returns the body to its pre-exercise state by gradually decreasing the pulse rate.

2 It helps to remove the waste products such as lactic acid produced during exercise.

3 The cool down is necessary for maintaining flexibility.

Components of a cool down

There are two components in a cool down:

1 Pulse lowering

Activities are required that gradually decrease in intensity and lower the pulse.

- Taking part in an active cool down helps to remove lactic acid at a faster rate than just stopping exercise.
- This means you are less likely to suffer from muscle soreness.
- Pulse lowering could involve slowing down from a run to a gentle jog, then to a fast walk and finally a slower walk.

2 Stretch

This involves maintenance and developmental stretches of the main muscles that were used in the activity session.

- Once you stop exercising, the muscles can remain in a slightly contracted state – a little shorter than before taking part in the exercise.
- This will eventually result in a decrease in flexibility and an increased risk of straining a muscle.
- Stretches are used in the cool down to return the working muscles to their resting length.

Types of stretching in a cool down

Maintenance and developmental stretches of different muscles are carried out in a cool down. See the table below.

Maintenance stretches are held for 15 seconds. They are used to maintain the length of a muscle rather than lengthen it.

This type of stretch is used for muscles where increased flexibility is not usually beneficial to sporting performance.

Maintenance	Developmental
• Deltoids	• Hip flexors
• Triceps	• Hamstrings
• Gastrocnemius	• Gluteus maximus
• Quadriceps	
• Obliques	• Erector spinae
• Abdominals	
• Biceps	

Developmental stretches are held for longer, usually around 30 seconds, to help lengthen the muscle and increase flexibility.

Now try this

Identify an activity that a person could take part in to lower their pulse.

Healthy diet

A healthy diet is necessary for our bodies to build and maintain tissues, and to carry out the functions that are needed to sustain life.

What is a healthy diet?

A healthy diet consists of:

- **macronutrients** (carbohydrates, fats and proteins), which are needed in large amounts in the diet
- **micronutrients** (vitamins and minerals), which are needed in very small amounts in the diet
- **liquids** to keep our bodies hydrated
- eating at least three meals a day.

Macronutrients

A healthy diet should include the right percentage of each macronutrient.

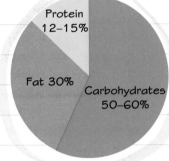

It can be beneficial to eat more of one type of macronutrient to improve sporting performance.

Revise macronutrients on pages 32–36.
Revise sports nutrition on page 40.

Calories

A calorie is a measurement of the energy available in food and drink – the more calories a food has, the more energy it will provide.

Calories are also referred to as kilocalories (kcal).

The recommended daily allowances (RDA) of calories are:

- men: 2500 kcal
- women: 2000 kcal.

The actual amount each individual needs varies according to age and activity levels:

- The more active a person is, the more energy they need in the form of calories to provide fuel for their activities.
- As a person gets older, after around age 40, they start to require fewer calories.

Micronutrients

Micronutrients are only needed in very small amounts by the body, but they are essential for good health.

The body is incapable of making most of the vitamins and minerals that it needs, so these must be supplied regularly in the diet.

- Vitamins are named using letters.
- Minerals are elements from the periodic table.

Revise vitamins and minerals on pages 37–38.

Hydration

Hydration is provided from the fluids we drink and the foods that we eat.

- Foods with high fluid content include fruits and vegetables.
- Most of your body is made up of water, so it is important to take in sufficient fluids each day to maintain our water balance and remain healthy.

Revise hydration and dehydration on page 39.

Now try this

Identify the recommended daily number of calories for:

1 adult males
2 adult females.

The Eatwell guide

The Eatwell guide provides a visual image of government recommendations for a balanced and healthy diet. Eating these foods in the correct proportions provides all the macronutrients and micronutrients that we need.

Carbohydrates

Carbohydrates should provide most of our calorie intake, making up around 50–60 per cent of our diet.

Structure of carbohydrates

Carbohydrate comes in two main forms: simple carbohydrates and complex carbohydrates. Fibre is also a form of carbohydrate.

* **Simple carbohydrates** consist of only one molecule. This means that they are quickly digested by the body and provide energy very quickly. These types of carbohydrates taste sweet.
* **Complex carbohydrates** are made up of many molecules and provide a slow release of energy. These types of carbohydrates do not taste sweet.

Excess carbohydrate in the diet is converted to and stored as body fat.

Function of carbohydrates

The main functions of carbohydrate are to provide energy for:

* the brain to function
* the liver to perform its functions
* muscular contractions at moderate to moderately high intensity.

Sources of carbohydrates

Simple carbohydrates contain mostly sugar.

Complex carbohydrates contain mostly starch and fibre.

A high-fibre diet

Fibre is found in wholegrain breakfast cereals, wholewheat pasta, wholemeal bread, brown rice, oats, vegetables, fruit, nuts and seeds.

Some complex carbohydrates contain fibre, which is necessary in the diet.

* The main function of fibre is to help prevent constipation and haemorrhoids.
* When fibre moves through the digestive system, it retains water which makes stools easier to pass.
* Fibre also helps to slow down how quickly the stomach empties and how quickly glucose enters the blood stream.

Now try this

1 Identify the two main types of carbohydrate.
2 Name a food that contains high levels of fibre.

Benefits of carbohydrates

Some sportspeople will benefit from consuming more carbohydrates than the average person because this macronutrient is beneficial for performance in aerobic endurance-based sports and activities.

Complex carbohydrates

When you exercise at a moderate to high intensity in aerobic activities, you use carbohydrates as the main energy source for muscle contractions.

- Complex carbohydrates are broken down slowly, so energy is released gradually over a long period of time.
- This is perfect for most aerobic activities, which usually last at least 30 minutes, as the carbohydrates will continue to supply energy for the duration of the activities.

Simple carbohydrates

Simple carbohydrates are broken down very quickly in the body – they enter the blood stream and are taken to the working muscles quickly.

- They can provide a boost of energy before a participant takes part in sport or activity.
- They can also be consumed during exercise because they are easy to digest and are therefore less likely to cause stomach upsets.
- When consumed after exercise, they help to replenish the body's carbohydrate stores that have been used up during exercise.

Exercising for longer than 90 minutes

Sports and activities that last longer than 90 minutes usually use up the body's stores of carbohydrates.

- Body fat could then be used as an energy source. However, it provides energy at a slower rate than carbohydrates, so the participant would have to exercise at a lower intensity, such as walking rather than jogging.
- To maintain a moderate to moderately high intensity, the participant should consume simple carbohydrates during their activity. This allows the body to continue using carbohydrates as the energy source.

Simple carbohydrate supplements

There are lots of simple carbohydrate supplements designed to be consumed by sports participants taking part in events that last longer than 90 minutes, such as marathons and triathlons.

- **Energy tablets** are chewed by the participant, and are often taken with water.
- **Energy drinks** contain high levels of carbohydrates in liquid form. These help with hydration as well as supplying simple carbohydrates.

Energy gels are available in single-serving packs. They have a sugary, gooey texture and can easily be swallowed by the participant while they continue to exercise.

Now try this

Explain why it is beneficial for a marathon runner to consume simple carbohydrates during their event.

- Think about how long (a) a marathon lasts, and (b) the body's stores of carbohydrates lasts.
- Also consider why simple carbohydrates are better than complex carbohydrates in this situation.

Protein

A healthy diet should consist of around 12–15 per cent of protein, depending on the specific needs of the individual.

Structure of protein

Protein is made up of amino acids. There are 20 amino acids in total. These amino acids can be split into two categories:

- **Essential amino acids:** there are eight essential amino acids. They are called essential because we must get them from food as the body cannot make them.
- **Non-essential amino acids:** there are 12 non-essential amino acids. They are called non-essential because the liver can make them if it has access to all the essential amino acids. It is therefore important that we eat all the essential amino acids every day.

Functions of protein

The main functions of protein are:

- to provide the building blocks that make up the structures of the body
- to allow the body to grow:

  from children into adults

  body tissue, especially muscle, in response to exercise
- to repair body tissues, such as muscle, ligaments and tendons, on a daily basis and after exercise.

Sources of protein

Protein is mainly found in foods of animal origin, but some plant-based foods are good sources of protein.

Good sources of protein include:

- **animal-based foods:** chicken, turkey, fish, lean beef
- **plant-based foods:** beans, nuts, seeds, meat substitutes such as Quorn.

Essential and non-essential amino acids

- **Complete proteins** are foods which contain all eight essential amino acids. Examples: chicken, eggs, fish, red meat, milk, cheese and soya beans.
- **Incomplete proteins** are foods which contain the non-essential amino acids. Examples: wheat, oats, rice, pulses, nuts, vegetables.

Soya beans are one of the very few sources of plant-based complete proteins. Most complete proteins come from animal sources.

Steak contains about 25% protein and 12% fat.

Now try this

1 State **two** functions of protein.
2 Explain what is meant by an essential amino acid.

Benefits of protein

Protein is required in the diet for people of all ages for growth and repair of body tissues. People who take part in exercise and sports that require high levels of strength will benefit from consuming higher quantities of protein than the average person.

Repairs body tissue after sport and activity

Repairs micro-tears in muscle tissue

Role of proteins in sport and activity

Promotes muscle growth

Promotes increase in strength

Promoting muscle growth and strength

- Strength training breaks down muscle fibres and produces micro-tears.
- The micro-tears stimulate the muscle tissue to repair itself and to grow slightly bigger, so it is more able to cope with the stress of the exercise.
- Further strength training continues to produce micro-tears and further growth of the muscle tissues.
- This growth is called muscle **hypertrophy**. Bigger muscles are able to produce more force, so the participant's strength increases.

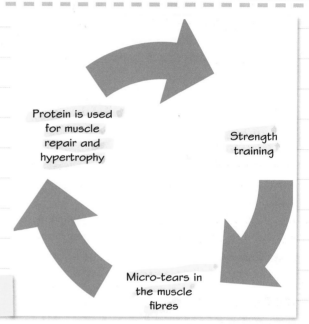

Protein is used for muscle repair and hypertrophy

Strength training

Micro-tears in the muscle fibres

The cycle of strength training and protein intake producing muscle hypertrophy

Tissue repairs

Other tissues in the body such as tendons and ligaments also need to be repaired after sport and activity.

- If a participant does not consume enough protein, these body tissues will not repair fully.
- The next time the participant takes part in physical activity, they are at greater risk of injury because the tissues might not be strong enough to withstand the stresses of the activity.

Milk and milkshakes are good post-exercise high-protein drinks.

Protein supplements

- Consuming protein foods and fluids straight after exercise helps to repair the micro-tears in muscle tissue at a faster rate than if is consumed later on after the activity.
- Supplements (such as protein shakes and bars) are portable and easy to consume straight after an activity.

Now try this

Simon takes part in regular weight training to improve his strength.

Explain why it is beneficial for Simon to consume a high-protein food straight after his weight-training session rather than a few hours later.

Fats

A healthy diet should contain around 30 per cent fat. No more than 10 per cent of our daily calories should come from unsaturated fats.

Structure of fats

Fats can be either saturated or unsaturated:

- **Saturated fats** consist of a long chain of carbon atoms. All the carbon atoms are attached to hydrogen atoms.

- **Unsaturated fats** also consist of a long chain of carbon and hydrogen atoms, but some hydrogen atoms are missing from the chain. Where the hydrogen atoms are missing, the carbon atoms attach to each other with double bonds.

Saturated fats have no double bonds between carbon atoms.

Unsaturated fats have one or more double bonds between carbon atoms.

Function of fats

Unsaturated fats are used as an energy source for:

- activities at low to moderate intensity such as walking

- our everyday functioning such as breathing, writing and standing up.

Saturated fats increase the total cholesterol in the body. Cholesterol is consumed in food and is also made in the body. Cholesterol is used for:

- building cell membranes

- helping the function of various hormones.

If there is too much cholesterol in the body, it can build up in the walls of arteries. This leads to an increased risk of coronary heart disease (CHD). Symptoms of CHD include angina (chest pain) and heart attacks.

Sources of fats

Saturated fats	Unsaturated fats
Usually come from animal sources	Come from plant and fish sources
<ul><li>Animal fats in red meat</li><li>Milk</li><li>Cheese</li><li>Cream</li></ul>	<ul><li>Salmon and other oily fish</li><li>Pumpkin seeds</li><li>Almonds</li><li>Walnuts</li><li>Avocado</li></ul>

Food preparation and fat content

- Fat can be added to foods during cooking. Frying and roasting both use added fat to cook the food and so can make low-fat foods become high in fat.

- For example, potatoes are low in fat, but after being deep fried to make chips, they have a high fat content.

Some methods of food preparation can reduce the fat content of foods. Grilling allows fat to drip off food such as meat during cooking.

Now try this

Explain how a diet high in saturated fat can increase the risk of coronary heart disease.

Vitamins

Vitamins are a type of micronutrient (a definition of micronutrients is given on page 31). Although our bodies only need tiny amounts of vitamins, they are vital to our health.

The main functions and sources of vitamins

Vitamin	Function	Sources
Vitamin A	Maintains normal eyesight, which is needed for hand–eye coordination and positional awareness	liver, mackerel, milk products, carrots, spinach
Vitamin B1	Helps convert food into energy which can be used for exercise	rice, bran, pork, beef, peas, beans, soya beans
Vitamin C	Maintains an effective immune system to prevent illness	most fresh fruit and vegetables
Vitamin D	Keeps bones, teeth and muscles healthy	oily fish, red meat, liver, egg yolks, mushrooms, **fortified foods**

A fortified food means that minerals and vitamins have been added to it. Types of foods that are often fortified include breakfast cereals and plant-based milk alternatives.

Water-soluble and fat-soluble vitamins

- Vitamins B1 and C are water-soluble. They cannot be stored in the body because any excess consumed is excreted in urine. We therefore have to eat foods containing these vitamins every day.
- Vitamins A and D are fat-soluble. This means they can be stored in the body's fat tissue. It is not necessary to consume foods containing these vitamins as regularly as the water-soluble vitamins.

Recommended daily allowance (RDA)

- We need to consume foods that are rich in vitamins every day, and there is an RDA for each vitamin.
- This is also referred to as the nutrient reference value (NRV).

We can achieve this by having a healthy and varied diet. Look at page 31 for a reminder of what this contains.

Vitamin supplements are also available. They can be useful when people have:

- a restricted diet, such as trying to lose weight
- dietary preferences, such as a vegan diet.

Benefits of vitamins in sport and activity

- Vitamin B1 aids the breakdown of food to convert it into energy, which is required for muscle contraction.
- Vitamin C helps maintain the immune system so it can fight bacterial infections. Having a strong immune system means that a participant won't have to take breaks in their training to recover from illness. They can become fitter and take part in their sport or activity regularly.

Vitamin A helps maintain good vision. It is essential for sports that require good hand–eye coordination and positional awareness.

Now try this

1 Identify **one** function of vitamin A.
2 State **one** food source that contains high levels of vitamin A.
3 Identify a water-soluble vitamin.

Minerals

Minerals are a type of micronutrient (this term is defined on page 31). As with vitamins, we need to regularly consume small amounts of minerals in our diet in order to maintain good health.

The main functions and sources of minerals

Mineral	Function	Sources
Potassium	Regulates body fluid levels to help ensure that we are hydrated during exercise	bananas, yoghurt, sunflower seeds, potatoes
Iron	Increases the body's oxygen-carrying capacity – this helps with aerobic performance by delivering oxygen to the working muscles	liver, lean meat, eggs, kidney beans, lentils, green vegetables such as spinach and broccoli
Calcium	Increases bone strength, which reduces the risk of injury in contact activities	milk and dairy products, whole grains, green vegetables

Benefits of minerals in sport and activity

- **Potassium** helps to maintain fluid and electrolyte balance levels during exercise. This helps to regulate body temperature.
- **Iron** produces red blood cells which carry oxygen around the body to the working muscles. This helps us run for long distances.
- **Calcium** increases the strength of bones. Strong bones are needed in all sports, but are especially useful in contact sports such as rugby, to prevent fractures.

During exercise, we sweat to help cool us down. Your body fluids contain potassium, which is lost when we sweat.

Absorption of micronutrients

Some food combinations help your body to maximise the absorption of micronutrients.

✓ Foods high in vitamin C help increase the absorption of iron from foods with a high iron content. However, consuming caffeine with foods that are high in iron will reduce the absorption of iron from the food.

✓ For bones to take in calcium and become stronger, the body also needs to have Vitamin D. These two micronutrients work together to increase bone strength.

Now try this

Explain why a triathlete needs to ensure that they have sufficient quantities of iron in their diet.

Hydration

Water is essential for our bodies to function. In fact, over half of the body is made up of water. It is therefore necessary to remain hydrated for our health and well-being.

How much water?

The recommended daily intake (RDI) of fluids is:

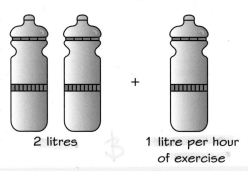

2 litres + 1 litre per hour of exercise

In hot environments and during exercise, more fluid intake will be needed. Additional fluid intake is necessary during and after exercise, because of the fluid lost through sweating.

Sources of fluids

Fluid is obtained from drinks, but it is also present in foods such as fruit. If you eat a lot of foods with a high water content, it is not always necessary to drink the full recommended daily intake.

While water is the cheapest and often the best source of rehydration, there are a range of sports drinks available:

✓ **Hypertonic** drinks are high in carbohydrates, so are useful for refuelling after exercise.

✓ **Isotonic** drinks contain some carbohydrates and provide the fastest hydration of the three types of sports drink.

✓ **Hypotonic** drinks contain very few or no carbohydrates, and just provide fluid replacement.

Benefits of hydration for sport and activity

Hydration lubricates the joints so that they can move freely during sport and exercise.

Hydration allows us to sweat. This helps prevent the body from overheating when exercising and maintains the normal body temperature (37°C).

Hydration makes the blood **plasma** (the liquid part of the blood) thinner, so it can work effectively and transport oxygen and nutrients to the muscles during sport and activity.

Dehydration

Dehydration is a harmful reduction of fluid in the body.

During exercise, dehydration can result from not replacing the fluids lost through sweating. Dehydration can decrease performance in sport and activity, and can be dangerous. During dehydration:

- the blood becomes thicker because the volume of blood plasma gets smaller
- the body sweats less, because sweat is produced mainly from the fluid in blood plasma
- the body temperature increases, as excess body heat cannot be lost through sweating.

Avoiding dehydration

Starting any exercise in a hydrated state helps to maximise performance.

- During exercise, drinks can be sipped at various stages, especially if the exercise session lasts for over 30 minutes.
- After the exercise session, it is very important to rehydrate fully by drinking liquids soon after completing the exercise session, and then further drinks when required.

Some drinks are unsuitable for rehydration, including those that contain caffeine or high levels of carbohydrates.

Now try this

1 State the recommended daily intake of fluids.
2 Explain **one** benefit of being properly hydrated for participation in sport or activity.

Sports nutrition

A healthy diet is important in maintaining optimal health and well-being. It is therefore vital for helping our bodies adapt after participation in sports and activity.

Nutrition for sport and activity

Everyone needs to have a healthy diet (look at page 31 for a reminder). A varied and healthy diet provides sufficient quantities of all the macronutrients and micronutrients that the body needs.

People who take part in sports and other physical activities need to make sure that their diet:

1 **replaces energy** lost during sport or activity – **carbohydrate** intake (pages 32–33).
Participants in endurance sports and activities should consume more carbohydrates (60 per cent) because they provide the main source of fuel for these activities.

2 **repairs damage** done to the body's structures during sport or activity – **protein** intake (pages 34–35).

3 **ensures correct functioning** of all the body's systems – **vitamin and mineral** intake (pages 37–38).

4 **maintains hydration** – **fluid** intake (page 39).

Areas for improvement

It is important to consume the correct amount of each macronutrient in our diet.

Carbohydrate	Fat	Protein
50–60%	30%	12–15%

Those who are making poor food choices will need to make changes to their diet. This could involve:

- eating the correct quantities of micronutrients, perhaps cutting down on fat or increasing protein intake
- increasing fluid intake
- increasing the number of meals to at least three meals a day.

Carbohydrate loading

We store carbohydrate in our muscles and liver in the form of glycogen. This store will only supply fuel for around 90 minutes to two hours of exercise at moderate to high intensity.

- Carbohydrate loading helps to increase the amount of carbohydrate a person can store.
- This is used by sportspeople such as marathon runners, who take part in aerobic events that last more than two hours.

Applying carbohydrate loading

- Reduce training three days before the event.
- Have complete rest the day before the event.
- Over this four-day period, consume 10–12 g of carbohydrate for every 1 kg of body weight.

What happens when carbohydrate stores run out?

The term 'hitting the wall' is used in marathon running.

- This is when a runner suddenly stops running and is only able to walk – they do not have any carbohydrate stores left to run any further.
- Their body does not have a source of energy that can provide fuel quickly enough to allow them to run.

Now try this

1 Identify a sport in which participants would benefit from carbohydrate loading.

2 Explain why carbohydrate loading is used by some sportspeople.

For question 1, try to think of a long-distance endurance sport where the participant is active for two hours or more.

Timing of food intake

Food is essential to provide fuel for participation in sport and activity. When some types of food are consumed at specific times, this can help to maximise performance.

What and when to eat

	When?	Type of food	Benefits
Before	The night before and/or the first few hours the next day	Complex carbohydrates	Ensures that the body's stores of carbohydrates are full
	Just before any sport, training or activity	Simple carbohydrates	Provides a quick supply of energy at the start of training, activity or event
During	When the person is exercising	Simple carbohydrates Fluids that contain carbohydrates	Provides energy Rehydrates
After	Within two hours of finishing the sport, training or activity	Protein	Repairs muscle fibres
		Carbohydrates	Restocks the body's supply of carbohydrates
		Fluids that contain carbohydrates	Rehydrates and provides a supply of carbohydrates

 ## Sample menu for participation in an exercise activity

The night before:

Pasta meal (complex carbohydrate)

Just before:

Jelly beans (simple carbohydrate)

During:

Energy gels and sports drinks (simple carbohydrate and fluid for hydration)

Milk (protein and fluid for hydration)

After:

A meal with chicken (protein), potatoes (carbohydrates) and vegetables (vitamins)

Bowel emptying

It is important to eat foods that are high in fibre because they:

- help with the digestion process
- allow us to empty our bowels and excrete waste products in a timely and comfortable manner.

A diet with low levels of fibre can result in constipation. Look at page 32 for a reminder of a high-fibre diet.

Now try this

Soraya takes part in strength training using free weights.

Explain which type of food Soraya should consume after finishing weight training.

Remember, strength training causes micro-tears in muscle fibres. Which macronutrient is used to repair muscle tissue?

Legal supplements

A legal supplement is one that sportspeople who compete at a high level can take when they are training and competing. The supplement has to be specific to the type of sport or activity in order to boost performance and reduce recovery time.

Vitamins B and D

- **Vitamin B** helps to convert food into energy. For sports and activities that require repeated muscular contractions for prolonged periods of time, vitamin B is essential in ensuring the muscles receive enough energy to keep going.
- **Vitamin D** helps to maintain bone and muscle health, which are vital for sport and activity performance. Our bodies can make their own vitamin D if we are exposed to enough sunshine.

When are vitamin supplements needed?

- Vitamin B is a water-soluble vitamin, so it cannot be stored in the body. Supplements might benefit participants in sports involving muscular endurance.
- Vegetarians and vegans might not consume enough Vitamin B and D in their diets. Vitamin D is found mainly in foods from animal sources.
- People who live in parts of the world with little sunshine during the winter months might benefit from taking a vitamin D supplement in the winter.

Other supplements

Type	Examples	What is it for?	👍 Advantages	👎 Disadvantages
Protein supplements	Protein shakes Protein bars	People who want to gain more muscle tissue and need to consume more protein than the average person.	Quick to consume. Convenient to use. Deliver high concentrations of protein, low levels of carbohydrates and little or no fat. Help reduce recovery time after exercise.	Usually made from a dry, powdered form of protein. This might damage the amino acids and affect how well the body can use them. Many contain sugars, sweeteners, colourings. Can be expensive.
Pre-workout supplements	Energy gels Glucose tablets Jelly beans	Provide a burst of energy that the person can use as soon as they start their workout or training session.	Contain high levels of carbohydrate, very little protein or fat. Easy and quick to consume. Cause little or no stomach discomfort. Help reduce recovery time after exercise.	After a short burst of energy, they can make a person feel very tired if not taking part in sport or activity, as the excess sugar is removed from the bloodstream.
Glucose-based isotonic drinks	Many different brands available	Help to rehydrate. Provide simple carbs for energy: 4–8 g of sugar per 100 ml fluid.	Similar concentration of dissolved solids as in blood so the body absorbs the fluid very quickly and is rehydrated. Help reduce recovery time after exercise.	High in calories and can lead to weight gain. Sugar in the drinks could contribute to tooth decay and weight gain.
Caffeine drinks	Coffee Cola drinks Sports drinks	Caffeine increases energy levels, concentration and alertness.	Can reduce perception of effort when taking part in sport or activity. Increase the use of fats as an energy source.	Possible side effects: insomnia, anxiety, diarrhoea, high blood pressure and energy peaks and troughs.

Now try this

Identify **one** advantage and **one** disadvantage of taking a caffeine supplement.

Motivation

Motivation can be defined as what drives people to behave in a particular way. We can be motivated to participate in sport or activity in many different ways.

Sports psychology and motivation

- **Psychology** is the study of the mind and how it affects behaviours.
- **Sport psychology** is the study of how the mind affects actions and performance when taking part in sport and activity.
- Sports psychologists study **motivation** because they want to understand what drives a person to want to continue participating and competing in their sport or activity.

Types of motivation

There are two types of motivation:

 Intrinsic motivation

A person is motivated by internal factors, not external rewards. The motivation to do something comes from how that action makes the person feel.

Examples of intrinsic motivation for taking part in sport or activity include:

- enjoyment of the sport or activity itself
- enjoyment from being with others in a sports club or team
- the challenge of progressing in the sport or activity
- the feeling of becoming fitter
- pride from attaining higher levels of achievement.

2 Extrinsic motivation

A person is motivated by external rewards for taking part or for doing well. The rewards can be tangible or intangible.

- **Tangible rewards** are physical rewards, such as money, a prize or a trophy.
- **Intangible rewards** are non-physical rewards, such as praise or recognition.

Examples of extrinsic motivation for taking part in sport or activity include:

- entering a competition because prize money is on offer
- praise from sports leaders, family members and friends
- public recognition for succeeding in a sport or event.

Intrinsic and extrinsic motivation

Many sportspeople are motivated by a combination of both intrinsic and extrinsic motivation.

☑ They want to perform well in an event because they gain feelings of pride as well as the adrenalin rush of competing.

☑ At the same time, they want to gain the recognition or prize that comes from winning.

Children might take part in a sports day race because they hope to win tangible rewards such as a medal.

Now try this

Nathan takes part in weekly five-a-side football games because he enjoys playing the game.

1. Identify the type of motivation that makes Nathan participate in the five-a-side football games.
2. Describe what is meant by a tangible reward.

Benefits of increased motivation

Increasing a participant's motivation has a positive effect on their performance in a sport or activity.

1 Higher intensity of effort

- A highly motivated person is able to push themselves harder and exercise at a higher intensity than a person with lower motivation levels.
- In training, a highly motivated person might be able to shut out feelings of fatigue and pain and work at maximum capacity during each training session.
- They are able to use their mind to drive them on to succeed.

2 Continuing to take part

- For health and fitness gains, participation in sport and activity should take place regularly each week.
- With work, study and other commitments, it can be difficult for people to fit training into a busy schedule.
- If someone's motivation levels are high enough and are maintained, this will help them to overcome reluctance to take part in training, and continue to participate on a regular basis.

3 Overcoming adversity

Adversity is a situation or experience that is upsetting or unpleasant.

- Examples of adversity in sport could include getting injured, performing badly in a competition or not being picked for a team.
- Adverse situations outside sport might also negatively impact a person's desire to participate in fitness – such as failing a test at school, falling out with a friend or finding out that a family member has been diagnosed with a serious illness.
- High levels of motivation can help a person to overcome adverse situations and make themselves continue to participate in training and competition.

4 Higher enjoyment levels

- High levels of motivation help a person to gain more enjoyment from participation in training and sports events.
- This is because they look forward to training as it is something that they know they will enjoy.
- They will be pleased to have completed the training as they will be experiencing the benefits of having participated.

Enjoying training sessions significantly increases motivation.

5 Increased intrinsic and extrinsic rewards

- Regular participation in sport and training brings increased intrinsic rewards. The participant will continue to enjoy the positive feelings they get from their sport or activity.
- In addition, they are more likely to benefit from extrinsic rewards. Their fitness levels and skills will improve through regular training, and they will be able to compete at a higher level.

Revise examples of intrinsic and extrinsic rewards on page 43.

Now try this

A cricket coach uses a range of methods to increase the motivation levels of his team.

State **two** benefits that the team might experience as a result of increased motivation.

Self-confidence

Self-confidence can be defined as having trust in yourself, and believing in your own ability to perform at your best and achieve your goals.

Why is self-confidence important?

Self-confidence can have a significant positive impact on a person's ability to succeed in sports-related situations. A high level of self-confidence is regarded as something to strive for.

Hockey players with high levels of self-confidence will try to get possession of the ball, to help their team play well.

1 Increased intrinsic motivation

- High levels of self-confidence are linked to high levels of motivation.
- Being highly motivated is beneficial. It increases a person's participation in training, which will improve their chances of success in the sport or activity.

You can revise intrinsic motivation on page 43.

2 Positive attitude

- An **attitude** is something that influences the actions a person chooses to take, and their responses to challenges.
- A **positive attitude** will increase a person's belief that they can achieve their goals. It is therefore very important to help motivate them to take part in the preparation and training required for sporting success.

3 Improved performance

- High levels of self-confidence give a person the belief that they are capable of performing at a high level. They will not feel inferior to other competitors.
- In team sports such as netball and football, a person with high levels of self-confidence will be an active member of the team.
- On the other hand, a person with low levels of confidence might avoid the ball, for fear of making a mistake and letting the team down.

4 Improved concentration and effort

- High levels of self-confidence allow a person to focus fully on the sport or activity.
- A person with low levels of self-confidence is likely to have doubts and concerns that distract them from their sporting performance.
- High levels of self-confidence help to increase the amount of effort a person puts in, which will also improve performance.

Now try this

Sanjay is taking part in a school rugby 7s tournament. He has high levels of self-confidence and is ready for the tournament.

1 State the definition of self-confidence.
2 Explain how Sanjay's high levels of self-confidence can help to improve his sporting performance.

Increasing self-confidence

Self-confidence is beneficial for an individual as well as their sporting performance (look at page 45 for a definition of self-confidence). There are several different methods that can be used to increase a person's self-confidence.

1 Positive reinforcement

- A sports leader can provide positive reinforcement such as rewards, praise and positive feedback, which are all forms of extrinsic motivation.
- Positive reinforcement can help increase a participant's self-confidence, because it shows that the sports leader recognises and acknowledges the participant's hard work or achievement of set goals.

Revise extrinsic motivation on page 43.

2 Positive environment

A positive environment is one in which people are not afraid to take chances, as they will not be criticised for making mistakes.

- A sports leader can create a positive environment using praise, enthusiasm, good-quality feedback and positivity.
- This will improve the participants' self-confidence, so that they are more likely to perform well, enjoy their sport or activity and continue to participate.

3 Training partner of similar ability

A training partner is someone who takes part in training with you.

- It is important that both participants are of a similar ability, so that they can keep up with each other and help each other to develop fitness and skills at the same pace.
- Being able to keep up with each other and progress together will help develop both partners' self-confidence.
- Having a training partner also helps a person to commit to training – they don't want to let their partner down, and might feel more confident than training on their own.

A training partner can help increase a person's self-confidence to participate in an activity because they are not alone.

4 Goal setting

A goal is something that a person wants to achieve.

- Goals can be short-term or long-term, and provide a person with something to aim for.
- Achieving a goal will increase a participant's self-confidence because they can see that they are progressing.

Goals should be SMART:

- Specific – must be stated clearly and be related to what the person wants to achieve.
- Measurable – able to be monitored.
- Achievable – the participant should be able to do it.
- Realistic – the participant must have enough time and suitable facilities to work towards their goal.
- Time-related – a set timescale to achieve the goal.

5 Self-talk

Self-talk means making positive statements to yourself, either out loud or in your head, in order to help you focus and keep on track.

- You can use self-talk in training and in competition.
- Self-talk can be very uplifting: someone who is feeling tired in competition or is making mistakes and needs to lift their game might say to themselves 'You can do this!' to increase their self-confidence to perform.

Now try this

Grace wants to get back into running to improve her fitness levels. She is worried because she hasn't been running for many years and has low levels of self-confidence.

Explain **two** methods Grace can use to improve her self-confidence levels so that she can start running.

Anxiety

Anxiety is the level of worry or nervousness experienced by a participant. Anxiety has a negative effect on sport performance and participation.

There are two main types of anxiety – state anxiety and trait anxiety.

1 State anxiety

State anxiety is related to the situation a person is in. State anxiety:

- is a short-term emotional state that can frequently change
- is a sportsperson's emotional response to a situation that they perceive as threatening, such as high-level competition where there is pressure to perform well
- varies and might only occur in specific situations.

Sources of state anxiety

State anxiety can come from many factors, such as:

- the environment being too noisy – for example, loud chants from the spectators might put someone off their game
- the environment being too quiet – this might make a participant think the spectators are not enjoying watching the event
- negativity from fellow competitors
- not managing to stick to the training schedule so not feeling properly prepared for the event.

2 Trait anxiety

Trait anxiety is related to a person's personality. People who have high levels of trait anxiety:

- can become worried, fearful or anxious in many situations
- view more situations as threatening than people with lower levels of trait anxiety
- are likely to respond to particular situations with higher levels of state anxiety.

Sources of trait anxiety

Trait anxiety can also come from many factors in our lives, such as:

- lack of sleep
- being a perfectionist
- being too self-critical
- low self-confidence
- unrealistic expectations – either your own or from other people such as family or friends.

Experiencing state anxiety

- At the start of an important cup final game, a player might have high levels of state anxiety, which then decrease once the whistle has blown and the game has begun.
- Their state anxiety levels might increase again at various times in the game, such as when the opposition scores or the player is required to take a penalty.

During a rugby cup final game, a player might experience high levels of state anxiety when they step up to kick a conversion.

Now try this

Laura takes part in swimming and is thinking about entering a swimming gala. However, the thought of competing against other swimmers makes her anxious.

Describe what is meant by trait anxiety.

Think of a 'personality trait' to help you remember that trait anxiety is related to a person's personality.

Effects of anxiety

Anxiety can have physical and psychological symptoms that affect our ability to perform well or take part in sport and activity.

Somatic anxiety

Somatic anxiety refers to the **physical effects** a person feels as a result of anxiety.

Examples of somatic anxiety are:

- butterflies in the stomach
- muscle tension
- increased heart rate
- increased sweating.

Effects of somatic anxiety

High levels of somatic anxiety can result in:

1. **Lack of coordinated movement** – focusing on negative feelings can lead to muscle tension, which makes it difficult for a person to move freely and fully control their actions.

2. **Aggression** – increased heart rate, muscle tension and adrenalin production might lead to foul play in game situations.

3. **Feeling unwell** – symptoms such as fluttering in the stomach might prevent a participant from being able to work at their maximum intensity or perform at their best.

② Cognitive anxiety

Cognitive anxiety refers to the **psychological effects** of anxiety. Think of it as 'worrying about something'.

Examples of cognitive anxiety include:

- feeling worried
- poor concentration levels
- lack of sleep due to overthinking.

Effects of cognitive anxiety

High levels of cognitive anxiety can result in:

1. **Negative mental state** – the participant feels high levels of worry and apprehension, which will affect their performance.

2. **Loss of self-confidence** – too much worry can make the participant believe they are not good enough to reach their goal. This will have a negative effect on performance.

3. **Lack of focus** – this can cause poor technique, mistakes and sustaining injuries or injuring other players.

Cognitive anxiety can cause lack of focus, resulting in mistakes such as a mistimed tackle.

Now try this

Explain the difference between somatic anxiety and cognitive anxiety.

Controlling anxiety

A sports or activity leader can use a number of techniques to help people control their anxiety, so that they can participate in sport and activity, receive more pleasure from their participation, and enjoy the benefits of competing in events.

The role of the sport or activity leader

People can feel anxiety in a number of situations:

- Someone who hasn't taken part in sport or activity for a long time can feel very anxious about taking the first steps. They might worry about looking silly, or feel they aren't good enough to join.
- Someone who already takes part in sport or activity might experience anxiety in certain situations, such as before a big event or competition.

The sports or activity leader is important in supporting participants to overcome their anxiety.

① Activities based on ability levels

Many fitness activities are grouped according to level of experience and ability, and level of fitness. Participants can often choose between levels such as beginners, intermediate and advanced.

- Being able to take part in an activity at the appropriate level helps reduce anxiety and increases participation, because people won't feel they are performing at a lower level than other members of the group.
- Exercise classes and sports leagues all use this principle.

② Fitness induction

A fitness induction is designed to familiarise new members with the facilities and equipment in a sport or health and fitness centre.

- This can help to overcome anxiety by removing fear of the unknown. After the induction, people will know where to go and how to use the equipment.
- The induction will help them to understand that the staff at the fitness centre are there to help and support them to overcome any anxieties.

A fitness induction helps make a new participant feel more comfortable with the gym facilities and staff.

③ Use of music

- Music can be very calming. If participants are anxious before an important game or competition, playing the right choice of tunes can help to relax them.
- Music can also be very energising and motivating. Playing upbeat music at group exercise classes (such as aerobics or spinning) will help to lower participants' anxiety levels, as they focus on moving to the music rather than any worries they might have about the class.

④ Pre-match team talk

Anxiety before a match or competition is very common. A sports leader or coach can give a sports team a pre-match talk to help increase their confidence levels and reduce anxiety.

- The talk should focus on positive aspects, such as the team's strengths, how good they must be to be taking part in the match, and how well they have trained.
- A positive team talk helps reduce anxiety by reassuring the participants that they are capable of doing well, both as individuals and as a team.

Now try this

Sian is an aerobics instructor and is teaching a new class for older adults. She puts together music tracks that would have been popular when the class participants were younger.

Remember that some music tracks motivate us to get out and do some exercise, or to work harder in a training session. Other tracks help to calm us down.

Explain how the music selected will help to reduce the anxiety of older adults taking part in this class for the first time.

Your Component 2 exam

Your Component 2 exam will be set by Pearson and could cover any of the essential content in the unit. You can revise the unit content in this Revision Guide. This skills section is designed to **revise skills** that might be needed in your exam. The section uses selected content and outcomes to provide examples of ways of applying your skills.

Exam checklist

Before your exam, make sure you:

✓ have a black pen that you like and at least one spare

✓ have a calculator and put in a new battery if your school does not provide one

✓ have double checked the time and date of your exam

✓ get a good night's sleep.

Check the Pearson website

The questions and sample response extracts in this section are provided to help you to revise content and skills.

Ask your tutor or check the Pearson website for the latest **Sample Assessment Material** and **Mark Scheme**, so that you know the structure of the paper and what you need to do. The details of the actual exam may change, so always make sure you are up to date.

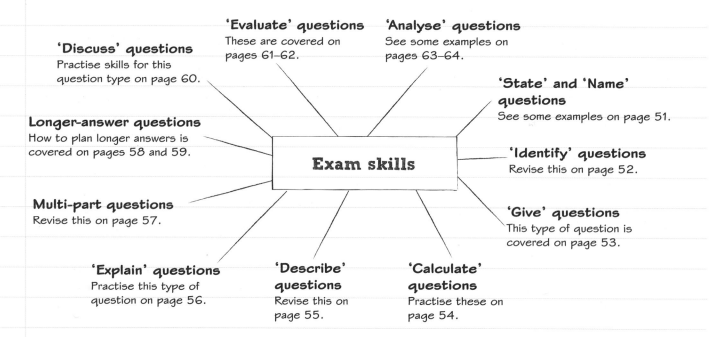

'Discuss' questions
Practise skills for this question type on page 60.

'Evaluate' questions
These are covered on pages 61–62.

'Analyse' questions
See some examples on pages 63–64.

'State' and 'Name' questions
See some examples on page 51.

Longer-answer questions
How to plan longer answers is covered on pages 58 and 59.

Exam skills

'Identify' questions
Revise this on page 52.

Multi-part questions
Revise this on page 57.

'Give' questions
This type of question is covered on page 53.

'Explain' questions
Practise this type of question on page 56.

'Describe' questions
Revise this on page 55.

'Calculate' questions
Practise these on page 54.

Now try this

Visit the Pearson website and find the page containing the course materials for BTEC Tech Award in Sport, Activity and Fitness. Look at the latest Component 2 Sample Assessment Material (SAM) for an indication of:

- whether the paper is in parts
- how much time is allowed
- how many marks are allocated
- what types of questions appear on the paper.

Your teacher may already have provided you with a copy of the Sample Assessment Material. You can use this as a 'mock' exam to practise before taking your actual exam.

'State' and 'Name' questions

When responding to a 'State' or 'Name' question, you need to give a definition or an example. This type of question is testing your knowledge of essential content in the specification. You should be able to recall the answer.

Izzy is a gymnast. She takes part in the vertical jump test.

(a) State the component of fitness tested by the Sargent jump test.   (1)

 Links Revise the Sargent jump test on page 7.

Sample response extract

Power

Keep your answers to 'State' and 'Name' questions simple. This learner has correctly named the component of fitness – there is no need to give any explanation or description.

Anita is a triathlete. During the cycling part of the race, she plans to have a sports drink, which is a type of legal supplement.

(b) Name a type of legal supplement that Anita could drink that would be beneficial to triathlon performance.   (1)

Always read the introduction text to each question. This sets the scene and may provide important information.

 Links Revise legal supplements on page 42.

Sample response extract

Glucose-based isotonic drink

Sometimes there could be more than one correct answer, so choose one that you are sure is right. This learner could also have said 'Caffeine drink', but was more confident with the answer here.

A healthy diet should include foods that contain a range of different micronutrients.

(c) State what is meant by a micronutrient.   (1)

 Links Revise the components of a healthy diet on page 31.

Some 'State' questions might ask you to give a meaning or definition.

Sample response extract

A vitamin

 Be careful when you are asked to give a definition. This answer has given an example of a micronutrient instead of the meaning.

Improved response extract

A micronutrient is a nutrient that is required in small quantities.

This answer is much better – it gives a clear definition of micronutrient. There is only one mark allocated here, so you don't need to go into too much detail.

Now try this

Tristan takes part in cross-country running, which requires high levels of aerobic endurance.

Name **two** methods of training that would help to improve Tristan's aerobic endurance.   (2)

 Choose two of the three types of aerobic endurance training you have learned about.

 Links You can revise training for aerobic endurance on page 9.

'Identify' questions

The command verb 'Identify' means that you need to assess factual information given in the question. It is usually enough to answer using one word or sometimes a few words, depending on the information given.

Jack is 17 years old and took part in the sit and reach test. His result was **13cm**.

Rating	Males (cm)	Females (cm)
Excellent	25+	20+
Very good	17	17
Good	15	16
Average	14	15
Poor	13	14
Very poor	9	10

Table 1

(a) Using **Table 1**, identify the category Jack is in for the sit and reach test. (1)

 You might be asked to identify information that is presented in a table or chart.

 This question text and table provide a lot of information, which might be needed in the question. You could quickly underline information that might be relevant.

 In this question you can deduce the gender (from the name 'Jack' and the word 'His'). You are also told Jack's age, but age is not relevant for the sit and reach test.

Sample response extract

Poor

 As the question just asks you to identify the category and there is only 1 mark, a one-word response is enough.

Links Find out more about the sit and reach test on page 4, and revise normative data on page 1.

Teni is a basketball player. The night before a big match, he finds he can't sleep and worries about how he is going to play the next day.

(b) Identify the type of anxiety that Teni has before a big basketball match. (1)

 You might be asked to identify what is being referred to in a definition or description.

It is important to use the correct term. You will need to recall this from your knowledge of the essential content.

Sample response extract

Cognitive anxiety

Links You can revise the effects of anxiety on page 48.

Now try this

Table 2 shows one week of Holly's training programme.

Day	Activity
Mon	25 min continuous training – running
Tues	Rest
Wed	25 min continuous training – running
Thu	Rest
Fri	25 min continuous training – running
Sat	30 min continuous training – running
Sun	Rest

Table 2

Identify which FITT principle is **not** included in Holly's training programme.

 Go through each of the FITT principles in turn (Frequency, Intensity, Time, Type) and check whether they have been included in the table.

 You just need to state the principle in your answer.

Links You can revise the FITT principles on pages 15–19

'Give' questions

Questions with the command word 'Give' might ask you to provide examples, definitions, justifications or reasons. You might need to write one word, a few words or a whole sentence, depending on the information required.

Michael plays tennis. Before a tennis competition, Michael is highly motivated to play as well as possible in each match.

(a) Give the definition of motivation. (1)

Sample response extract

Motivation is the internal mechanism and external stimuli that direct behaviour.

There is often more than one correct way of stating a definition. Here are other correct definitions:

- 'The internal and external factors that make people behave in a particular way'
- 'The reasons why we want to participate in sport or activity.'

(b) Give **one** example of how Michael's high level of motivation could benefit him in the tennis competition. (1)

Questions that ask for examples will state how many examples you should give.

Sample response extract

Michael's motivation is likely to make him try harder in the competition.

This answer is clear and to the point, and it contains all the relevant information.

 **Links** You can revise motivation on pages 43–44.

Tahani is a sprinter who suffers from anxiety before she takes part in 100m races.

(c) Give **two** negative effects of having high levels of anxiety on Tahani's participation in the 100m races. (2)

 Links You can revise the effects of anxiety on page 48.

Sample response extract

1. She may suffer from state anxiety which is anxiety related to a particular situation.
2. She may also suffer from trait anxiety which is where a person's personality makes them more tense and anxious.

Make sure you understand what the question is asking for. This question asks for negative effects of anxiety, not for definitions of the two types of anxiety. This answer would not gain any marks.

Improved response extract

1. She may have increased muscle tension.
2. She may have poor concentration levels.

This is a good response as increased muscle tension could negatively affect 100m sprinting performance.

This is another correct answer, as sprinters need to have good concentration to focus on the race.

Now try this

Brian takes part in marathon running events. He makes sure he eats plenty of complex carbohydrates in his diet before a marathon event.

 **Links** You can revise carbohydrates on pages 32–33.

Give **one** reason why complex carbohydrates are important in Brian's diet before his marathon events.

'Calculate' questions

Questions with the command word 'Calculate' require you to use your mathematical skills. In order to carry out a calculation, you will usually need to recall information from the essential content.

Remi is 20 years old and wants to lose excess body fat to improve his health. His personal trainer has advised him to exercise in the fat-burning training zone.

(a) Calculate the upper and lower limits of the fat-burning training zone for Remi. (3)

> There are several steps needed in the calculation for this question.

Sample response extract

Remi's Max HR = 220 − 20 = 200 bpm

Fat-burning zone: 60–70% Max HR

Lower heart rate: 60/100 × 200 = 120 bpm

Upper heart rate: 70/100 × 200 = 140 bpm

 1 First you need to calculate Remi's maximum heart rate, using the formula:

220 − age = Max HR

 2 You need to recall the percentages of Max HR for the fat-burning training zone.

 3 Then you need to calculate the lower and upper limits for his heart rate in this zone.

 Links You can revise intensity of training on page 17 and training zones on page 25.

> Make sure you show your working out. Even if you do get the wrong answer, you can still score a mark for using the correct method.

During a training session, Manpreet's personal trainer asks her to state her rate of perceived exertion using the Borg RPE scale. Manpreet tells her personal trainer that she is working at level 13.

(b) Calculate an estimate of Manpreet's heart rate when her RPE is 13. (2)

 Links You can revise the Borg scale and the rate of perceived exertion (RPE) scale on page 17.

Sample response extract

RPE × 10 = heart rate

13 × 10 = 130 bpm

> Here, you need to recall that multiplying the score by 10 will give you the estimated heart rate.

> Then you can carry out the calculation needed.

Now try this

> For question 1, you need to recall information from the essential content.

Julian is an adult male. He wants to ensure he is eating the correct number of calories per day. Table 1 shows the calories he consumes in one day.

Meal	Breakfast	Lunch	Dinner	Snacks
Calories	520	830	750	200

Table 1

> For question 2, first add up all of Julian's calories: 520 + 830 + 750 + 200. Then compare this to your answer to question 1.

1　State the recommended daily calorie intake for an adult male. (1)

2　Calculate whether Julian's calorie intake is higher or lower than the recommended daily intake. (2)

 **Links** Your answer to question 2 will depend on your answer to question 1. You can revise more questions with linked parts on page 57.

'Describe' questions

Questions with the command verb 'Describe' might ask you to give details about a key concept from the essential content, or to provide an account of a process.

Haniya is training to take part in a 5km cross-country run. She includes continuous training in her training programme to help prepare for the event.

(a) Describe what is meant by continuous training. (2)

 Links You can revise continuous training on page 9.

 You will usually need to write a whole sentence for a 'Describe' question in order to provide enough detail.

Sample response extract

Continuous training is where a person exercises at a steady pace for a period of at least 30 minutes.

 This response includes good details about continuous training, including what is involved and how long it should last for.

Sheldon takes part in hurdling. To help improve his performance, he carries out static stretching so that he is able to get into the right position to cross the hurdle quickly.

(b) Describe how to carry out static stretching. (2)

 Links You can revise static stretching and other types of flexibility training on page 11.

Sample response extract

To carry out a static stretch, you need to get your body into the correct position and stretch.

 This response is a good start to answering the question, but it needs to give more details about the process involved.

Improved response extract

Get the body into the correct position to stretch the targeted muscle or muscle group, and hold the position for 12–30 seconds.

This response gives a complete answer to the question:
- It describes the process involved in doing a static stretch.
- It includes relevant details, including what you need to do and how long for.

Now try this

Katya's personal trainer has used the principles of training to design a training programme for her. Progressive overload is one of the principles of training.

 Links You can revise progressive overload on page 21.

Describe what is meant by progressive overload.

'Explain' questions

The command verb 'Explain' might ask you to make a statement and justify it, or to name an example and give a reason why it is important or relevant.

Sanjit runs weekly after-school sports sessions at a local primary school. He would like to increase the children's motivation so that they try to focus more on the session.

(a) Explain **one** type of motivation Sanjit could use to help to increase the children's motivation in his sessions. (2)

 Always read the text that sets the scene for the question. It will help you to understand the situation.

Sample response extract

Sanjit could use extrinsic motivation, which means providing rewards for taking part or for doing well.

 This response starts well by naming a type of motivation. However, instead of **describing** what extrinsic motivation is, this learner should **explain** why it is appropriate.

Improved sample extract

Sanjit could use extrinsic motivation because children usually respond well to this type of motivation, in the form of rewards such as certificates or stickers.

 This is a better response because it names one of the two types of motivation, and gives a good reason why this would be appropriate for Sanjit to use for motivating children.

 Answers to 'Explain' questions often contain the words 'because' or 'so'.

 Links You can revise the two types of motivation (intrinsic and extrinsic) on page 43.

Hannah makes sure that she is fully hydrated before and during sports participation.

(b) Explain **one** reason why it is important for Hannah to be fully hydrated before and during participation in sport. (2)

 Links You can revise the benefits of hydration on page 39.

Sample response extract

It is important so that she can sweat and her joints can be fully lubricated.

 This response gives **two** reasons why hydration is important, but that is not what the question is asking for. This question requires just **one** reason and an explanation, so the statement about joints is not needed.

Improved response extract

It is important so that she can sweat, which will help avoid overheating during exercise.

 This response gives a complete answer:
• It gives one relevant reason.
• It explains why that reason is important.

Now try this

 Start by stating what the main function of iron is. Then give the benefit of this for sporting performance.

Penny is a long-distance runner. Her coach has advised her to eat more iron-rich foods in her diet to help improve her long-distance running performance.

Explain why more iron in Penny's diet might help improve her long-distance running performance.

 Links You can revise the role of minerals in sporting performance on page 38.

Multi-part questions

Some questions in your Component 2 exam might have several parts that are based on a scenario about a particular person and their sport or activity.

> Hussein is a keen footballer, who takes part in regular fitness training. Hussein wants to apply the FITT principles to his training.
>
> (a) (i) Identify which FITT principle is represented by the letter F.   (1)

 All the parts of the question will be based on the given scenario.

Sample response extract

> Frequency

> (ii) State how to apply this principle to a training programme.   (1)

> Set the number of training sessions each week.

 Some questions will require you to give linked answers. In this question, the answer to part (ii) will be based on your answer to part (i).

> Hussein wants to increase his self-confidence, because he knows that self-confidence can have an impact on his participation in his sport.
>
> (b) Give **one** benefit of self-confidence for participation in sport and activity.   (1)

 Always read the introduction to a new section of a question, as this will set the context and point to which parts of the essential content you need to recall.

 The command verb and the number of marks will tell you how much detail you need to give for each part.

Sample response extract

> It can improve concentration and effort.

> (c) Complete Table 1 by:
>
> (i) stating **two** methods that Hussein could use to increase his self-confidence.   (2)
>
> (ii) explaining how each of your chosen methods helps to increase self-confidence.   (2)

 For question (c), you need to give an example followed by an explanation.

 Make sure that each answer you give in part (ii) refers to the examples you have given in part (i).

(i) Method of increasing self-confidence	(ii) Explanation of how this increases self-confidence
Self-talk	Saying things to himself such as 'You can do it!' will lift his mood and make him feel more positive about himself.
Setting goals	Achieving his goals will help Hussein to progress in his sport, which will build his self-confidence.

Table 1

 **Links** You can revise self-confidence on pages 45–46.

Now try this

> Ace is a personal trainer. She uses a person-based approach when designing fitness programmes for her clients.
>
> **a** State **one** type of information that Ace needs to gather from each client so that she can design a personalised fitness programme for them.
>
> **b** Give **one** method she could use to gather this information.

 Links You can revise gathering information for a fitness programme on page 26.

Planning your responses to longer-answer questions

Some questions in your Component 2 exam will require longer answers. The command verbs for these questions include 'Discuss', 'Evaluate' and 'Analyse'. Revise these question types on pages 60–64.

Allow yourself some time to plan your answers to longer-answer questions, to make sure you can structure them well and don't leave anything important out.

Daphne is a long-distance swimmer. She is training for a 3 km open-water swim which will take place in six weeks' time.

Table 1 shows Daphne's weekly training programme.

Day	Training
Mon	60 minutes continuous training – swimming lengths of pool
Tues	60 minutes circuit training – land-based using low weights
Wed	30 minutes sprint training – sprint swims in the pool
Thu	60 minutes continuous training – swimming lengths of the pool
Fri	60 minutes free weight training – land-based using heavy weights
Sat	60 minutes continuous training – swimming lengths of the pool
Sun	30 minutes sprint training – sprint swims in the pool

Table 1

Discuss the suitability of Daphne's training programme to prepare her for the 3 km open-water swim. **(9)**

Points to remember for longer-answer questions

✓ Refer to all the information provided, including any tables.

✓ Consider all the different aspects of the situation, such as the positives and negatives.

✓ Show your knowledge and understanding of the Component 2 content.

✓ Only include information that is relevant to the question being asked.

✓ Use key terms correctly.

✓ Make links between different pieces of information.

✓ You might need to draw conclusions or make recommendations based on all the points you have made.

The key word in this question is 'Discuss'. You will need to explore in detail how well the training programme will help prepare Daphne for the event.

Sample notes extract

Intro:

- Types of fitness Daphne will need – muscular and aerobic endurance

Positives:

- Continuous training (20 min+) → aerobic endurance: 3 km swim = aerobic event
- Circuit training low weights → muscular endurance: 3 km swim = repeated muscle contractions

Negatives:

- Free weight training heavy weights → muscular strength: not necessary
- Sprint training → increased speed: not necessary
- 0 rest days → overtraining/injury

Organising your notes under headings will help you to structure your answer into paragraphs.

These notes clearly identify the positives and negatives of Daphne's training programme.

Make sure you show your understanding of the key concepts. These notes make links between each type of training and the component of fitness it is designed to improve.

The sample notes continue on the next page.

Planning your responses to longer-answer questions (continued)

The example notes extract starts on page 58 and continues below.

<u>Summary:</u>

- Well-planned programme
- Strength and speed training not necessary
- Add rest days to allow recovery and adaptations to training.
- 1 more continuous training session – more aerobic endurance

You won't have much time to plan in the exam, so your plan doesn't need to be as detailed as this one. You could:

- write a quick list of key words
- annotate the question and table instead
- use abbreviations, but make sure that you understand them.

 Links Revise the principles of specificity and overtraining on pages 20 and 22.

Links Revise training for the different components of fitness on pages 9–14.

Now try this

Write a **brief plan** to help you answer the 'Discuss' question below. (You will be writing a full answer to this question on page 60.)

Tom is training for a 10km cross-country race which is due to take place in six weeks.

Table 2 shows his training programme.

Day	Training	Intensity (% Max HR)
Mon	circuit training	60%
Tues	continuous training	70%
Wed	anaerobic hill sprints	70%
Thurs	continuous training	60%
Fri	continuous training	70%
Sat	circuit training	60%
Sun	rest	

Table 2

Discuss the suitability of Tom's training to develop his cross-country running performance.   (9)

 Consider each type of training in turn. Which component of fitness does it develop? Is this appropriate for Tom's event?

 Look at **all** the information you are given. Is the intensity appropriate for each training method?

 Are there any other aspects of the programme that you need to discuss (such as the rest day)? Is there anything missing (such as time, progressive overload)?

 Links You will need to bring together knowledge from different parts of Component 2:

- training for different components of fitness (pages 9–14)
- FITT principles and principles of training, particularly intensity (page 17) and training zones (page 25).

 In your plan list the positives of the training programme, the negatives and the points you should include in your summary.

'Discuss' questions

When answering 'Discuss' questions, make sure you consider all the different aspects of the situation you are given. Look back at the question and table on page 58, and the learner's plan, for a response. Then read the learner's completed response below. The annotations will help you understand what makes this response effective.

Sample response extract

To compete in a 3 km open-water swim, Daphne's training programme will have to develop her aerobic and muscular endurance.

Continuous training will improve Daphne's aerobic endurance. This component of fitness is necessary to be able to swim 3km, as this is an aerobic event. Continuous training needs to last at least 20 minutes to develop aerobic endurance – Daphne spends twice as long as this minimum time, which will help develop her aerobic endurance to keep swimming the full 3km distance.

 Make links between the information given in the question and your knowledge of the issues. One of the links made in this answer is the relevance of continuous training for the 3km swim event.

Circuit training will develop Daphne's muscular endurance as she uses low weights. Her muscles will have to keep contracting for long periods of time to keep swimming for 3 km, so training for muscular endurance is beneficial for her event.

 A well-developed discussion will consider the different aspects of the question. In this case, the learner explores both the positives and negatives of Daphne's programme.

There are some negative areas of her training programme. First of all, she doesn't have a rest day, which is very important to help prevent overtraining and reduce the risk of injury.

 Show accurate knowledge and understanding of the essential content. This answer shows understanding of overtraining and of the purposes of strength training and sprint training.

She also has some training sessions that aim to develop muscular strength using heavy free weights, and to develop speed using sprint training. These components of fitness are not very important for a 3 km long-distance swim.

 Make sure your discussion is clear and logical. This answer considers each of the main aspects of the programme in turn. It doesn't jump about between issues.

A well-planned training programme is very important to prepare Daphne for the 3 km open-water swim. Continuous training and circuit training are both good for improving the aerobic and muscular endurance that Daphne needs. Daphne doesn't need the free weight and sprint sessions. Instead, she should have one or two rest days to allow her body time to recover and to adapt to the training sessions already completed. She could add in another continuous training session to help maximise her performance in the 3 km swim.

 This learner has finished by summarising the key points they have made in their answer.

Now try this

Look at the 'Discuss' question at the bottom of page 59 and the plan that you wrote for this question.

Use your plan to write a full answer to the 'Now try this' question on page 59.

 Look back at the tips for longer-answer questions on page 58.

'Evaluate' questions

When answering 'Evaluate' questions, you need to consider both sides of a given situation or compare two options. You will need to examine the strengths and weaknesses or advantages and disadvantages, and finish by making a judgement. Remind yourself of the tips for longer-answer questions on page 58.

Andy takes part in triathlon events, which involve a 1500 m swim, a 40 km cycling race and a 10 km run. Before he takes part in a triathlon, Andy has the option of having a sports drink with high levels of caffeine or a glucose-based isotonic drink.

Evaluate which type of sports drink Andy should choose to benefit his performance in the triathlon.   (9)

Always read the scenario text carefully. You may not have studied a particular sport or activity in detail, so the scenario could give you valuable information to help you.

 Links You can revise the effects of legal supplements on page 42.

This question is asking for the pros and cons of drinking caffeine drinks and glucose-based isotonic drinks, and should finish with a judgement about which will benefit Andy the most.

Sample response extract

Caffeine can have several benefits for triathlon performance. It reduces a participant's perception of effort during sport or activity. This might help Andy to exercise at a higher intensity, allowing him to swim, run and cycle at a faster pace.

Caffeine increases the use of fats as an energy source. As the triathlon is an aerobic endurance event, it uses mainly carbohydrates to produce energy. The body can only store enough carbohydrate to last around two hours of continual exercise at moderate intensity. If fat is also used as an energy source, this will spare Andy's carbohydrate stores.

However, caffeine can have negative side effects such as insomnia, anxiety, diarrhoea and high blood pressure. If Andy suffered from any of these, it could harm his performance or even prevent him from taking part.

Glucose-based isotonic sports drinks can also have benefits for triathlon performance. This type of drink is absorbed quickly by the body, so the glucose concentrations in the blood will quickly increase. The glucose can be used to produce energy for Andy's muscles to contract at moderate to high intensity, to help him move at pace during the different phases of the triathlon.

As the body can only store a limited quantity of carbohydrates, taking on more glucose prior to the race will spare the carbohydrate stores so that they can be used later in the race to produce energy.

Make links and give explanations in your longer answers.

This answer starts by making links between each effect of caffeine and its possible impact on Andy's performance in the triathlon.

It fully explains each point that is made.

Always give the negatives as well as the positives for each option.

Make sure you explore each option in detail. Here, the learner has evaluated glucose-based isotonic drinks in the same detail as caffeine drinks.

 The answer continues on the next page.

'Evaluate' questions (continued)

The example evaluate question starts on page 61 and continues below.

The glucose-based drink will help to hydrate Andy prior to the race, which is important for sports performance.

However, the glucose-based isotonic sports drink will only provide carbohydrates at the start of the race, so Andy will need more drinks later in the race to maintain blood glucose levels.

To conclude, the glucose-based isotonic sports drink is the better option as it provides energy, hydrates Andy and has no real negative side effects. In contrast, the possible negative effects of caffeine could adversely affect Andy's performance.

Make sure your answer is relevant. Here, the learner relates every point they make to Andy's performance in the triathlon.

You will usually need to finish your answer to an 'Evaluate' question with a conclusion. This should:
- make a judgement
- give a direct answer to the question
- be supported by evidence from the rest of your answer.

Now try this

Alicia is 15 years old and is a sprinter. She will be competing in the 100 m at the schools district athletics competition in eight weeks' time. She does not feel confident about her ability to do well in the athletics competition.

Evaluate which methods Alicia should use to increase her self-confidence, both during training and at the athletics competition.

🔗 **Links** Revise methods to increase self-confidence on page 46.

Make a plan for this question. This could include the following headings:
- Intro: methods to increase self-confidence
- Training with partner, pros + cons
- Goal-setting, pros + cons
- Self-talk, pros and cons
- Other methods
- Conclusion

Try and add some further notes to these headings to help your answer.

'Analyse' questions with stimulus material

An 'Analyse' question might be based on information provided, for example in a table. You will need to examine and interpret the information in detail in order to answer the question. See also the tips for longer-answer questions on page 58.

Steve is a <u>basketball player</u>. He takes part in <u>strength training</u> to help improve his basketball performance.

Table 1 shows his food intake on a typical day.

Breakfast	Lunch	Dinner
• Wholemeal toast • Butter and jam • Fruit • Black coffee	• Baked potatoes • Tuna fish • Salad with avocado • Chocolate cake • Glass of water	• Pasta with tomato sauce and broccoli • Small chocolate bar • Orange juice

Table 1

<u>Analyse</u>, using **Table 1**, how Steve's intake of <u>protein, fat and carbohydrate</u> in his diet could <u>affect his basketball-playing performance</u>.　　(9)

You can underline the important parts of the scenario and question text to make sure you cover everything that is important in your answer.

This question asks you to focus on the three macronutrients in Steve's diet. You could annotate the table with details of the nutrients that each meal contains.

 Links You can revise the functions and sources of protein on page 34, and the benefits of protein for sport and activity on page 35.

Sample response extract

A healthy diet should contain around 12–15 per cent protein, 50–60 per cent carbohydrate and 30 per cent fat.

Steve's diet is very high in carbohydrate and very low in protein – the only protein-rich food he eats is tuna fish, in just one meal. Steve's intake of protein must be lower than the recommended amount. He also has a low fat intake.

Protein is essential for growth and for repair after exercise. Steve needs to consume protein because he takes part in strength training, which causes micro-tears in muscle fibres.

However, with so little protein in his diet, Steve's muscle fibres may not be able to fully repair after strength training. This will make his muscle fibres weaker, and there is more chance that he could get injured when playing basketball.

Steve needs high levels of carbohydrate to produce energy for the moderate to high intensity exercise involved in playing basketball: running, dribbling, marking players, shooting, and so on. Steve eats foods that are rich in complex carbohydrates at every meal. The complex carbohydrates in bread, pasta and potatoes will provide him with plenty of energy.

You could start your answer with a general statement like this one, which sets out what the learner will be comparing Steve's diet to.

Follow up any general statement by applying it to the situation and information given in the question.

This paragraph also starts with a general statement, this time about the function of protein. It goes on to apply this knowledge to Steve's situation.

You will need to draw on knowledge from different parts of the essential content and make links between them. Here, the learner has made links between protein, strength training, micro-tears and the chance of injury.

'Analyse' questions require a detailed response. Here, the learner explains why complex carbohydrates are important for Steve's sport.

 The answer continues on the next page.

'Analyse' questions with stimulus material (continued)

The example analyse question starts on page 63 and continues below.

Fat is required for energy production during low intensity exercise. Too much saturated fat in the diet can be harmful to health, as it can contribute to coronary heart disease.

Steve's diet probably consumes the right amount of fat. His diet does not contain red meat and it contains very few dairy products, so there is probably very little saturated fat in his diet. He eats healthy unsaturated fats in the form of avocados and tuna fish.

In conclusion, Steve is probably eating the right amount of carbohydrates to provide energy to play basketball. He also eats enough healthy unsaturated fat to keep him fit and healthy for his sport. However, Steve's low protein intake will adversely affect his muscle health and strength. This will have a negative effect on his basketball performance, so he needs to improve this aspect of his diet.

Make sure you cover all aspects of the question. Protein and carbohydrate might seem like the most important nutrients for Steve, but the question also asks the learner to analyse his fat intake.

Make sure your answer includes a direct answer to the question in your response. Here, the learner clearly states the overall effect of Steve's intake of all three macronutrients on his sport.

Now try this

Jan is a gymnast. She is working with her coach to devise a training programme to help to improve her fitness for gymnastics.

An example of the components of fitness to be trained each week is shown in **Table 1**.

🔗 **Links** You can revise the four FITT principles on pages 15–19.

Day	Component of fitness to be trained	Training method	Duration of session	Intensity
Mon	power	plyometrics	30 min	high
Tues	flexibility	static stretching	30 min	moderate
Wed	strength	resistance machines	30 min	high
Thu	power	plyometrics	30 min	high
Fri	flexibility	static stretching	30 min	moderate
Sat	strength	resistance machines	30 min	high
Sun	Rest			

Table 1

Analyse how the FITT principles are being used to plan Jan's fitness training in order to improve her gymnastics performance.

When you plan your answer, you could organise it by writing a paragraph about each of the FITT principles.

Focus your answer on the key points in the question:
- How has each FITT principle been applied in Jan's training programme?
- How will this help to improve her gymnastics performance?

Answers

The answers provided here are examples of possible responses. In some cases, other answers may also be possible.

1 Fitness testing

1. The protocol is the set method for carrying out the fitness test. It includes how the test is set up, which equipment should be used, how to complete the test correctly and how to record the results accurately.
2. The graph shows the measurements from a population. The highest point of the graph is in the middle because most people's results fall in the middle.
3. Gender and age.

2 Aerobic endurance

1. Below average.
2. Molly's score is probably not a true reflection of her aerobic endurance. She competes in swimming at county level, which is high-level sport. As a long-distance swimmer, she probably has high levels of aerobic endurance as this is needed to supply her working muscles with oxygen and nutrients when taking part in long-distance races. The test requires the participant to run, but Molly may not be used to running; therefore, she did not score well in the test as it did not replicate the same activity she uses when taking part in her sport.

3 Muscular endurance

1. Muscular endurance.
2. Poor.

4 Flexibility

1. Excellent.
2. Good.

5 Speed

1. (a) Above average.
   (b) Excellent.
   (c) Poor.
2. (a) A triathlete needs high levels of aerobic and muscular endurance. Although speed is not a key component of fitness required for the sport, a triathlete does need speed to be able to sprint past a competitor. Therefore, above average levels would be expected.
   (b) A 100 m sprinter needs high levels of speed as this event requires the athlete to be faster than the competitors. Therefore, an excellent rating would be expected.
   (c) A shot putter does not need to run quickly in their sport at all. They just need to have high levels of upper body strength to throw the shot a long distance. Having a poor rating for speed would be acceptable for this athlete.

6 Strength

The test only measures the strength of the hand and forearms, so does not provide information about the strength of other parts of Ola's body such as her legs.

7 Power

1. The vertical jump test is a good measure of power for a high jumper as it measures power in the legs. A high jumper requires high levels of power in their legs in order to jump as high as possible to clear the bar.
2. The test is not a good measure of power for a discus thrower, as a discus thrower needs high levels of power in their arms. The Sargent jump test only measures power in the legs. A high level of power in the legs is not needed to perform well in the discus.

8 Body composition

Excess body fat would increase the hurdler's body weight; they would have more weight to lift and would therefore have to work harder to jump high enough to clear the hurdles.

9 Training for aerobic endurance

One answer from the following:
- Torin can increase resistance by wearing a weighted back pack or by running uphill. This will increase the weight he is having to carry when he is running, and will make him work harder.
- Torin can increase the intensity by sprinting. This will make him work beyond the 80 per cent Max HR during the high-intensity periods.

10 Training for muscular endurance

Anita should use a high number of reps and low weights.

11 Training for flexibility

1. Static stretching and dynamic stretching.
2. PNF stretching helps to develop flexibility at a faster rate than other types of flexibility training.

12 Training for speed

Speed, agility and quickness (SAQ) training is a good choice. This type of training can be made sport-specific; Freddie can practise changing direction while sprinting and carrying a rugby ball, which is required when playing rugby.

13 Training for strength

Fixed resistance machines would be the best form of strength training for Molly because there is less chance of her getting injured than with free weights.

14 Training for power

Individual responses could include these points:
- Cathy can use targeted exercises for the muscle groups in her legs to improve their ability to generate power for jumping in a basketball game.
- The equipment is cheap and relatively easy to set up.
- Cathy can perform plyometrics exercises alone, at times that suit her schedule.

15 The FITT principles

1. Frequency, intensity.
2. Frequency: for example, three times per week.
   Intensity: for example, 60 per cent Max HR; moderate intensity

16 Frequency

1. Three sessions per week.
2. Four times per week – before and after every training session.

17 Intensity

1. 202 bpm.
2. 141 bpm.
3. 162 bpm.

18 Type

Individual responses could include:
1. Plyometrics.
2. She could take part in bouncing exercises where she jumps off a bench onto the ground and straight back up onto another bench. Other types of plyometric training exercises include hopping, lunging, press-ups with a clap, passing a medicine ball to a partner.

19 Time

1 Individual responses could include cycling, jogging, circuit training or any other type of activity used to develop aerobic endurance or muscular endurance.
2 Sean should exercise for at least 28 minutes.

20 Principles of training: specificity

Individual responses might vary but could include the following:
- Ryan could take part in rowing on a river to improve his fitness for rowing.
- He could use a rowing machine in a gym.

21 Progressive overload

Progressive overload means gradually increasing the participant's workload over time to achieve an improvement in their fitness.

22 Overtraining

Individual responses might vary. Overtraining might be the reason that Yang's fitness levels are not improving. He might not be allowing his body enough time to adapt to the training.

23 Reversibility

Individual responses might vary. Possible answers include injury or illness that prevents them training, or a holiday where there are no training facilities.

24 Differences and needs

Individual responses might vary.
1 Speed and power.
2 Sprint training would be beneficial because Jardine has to be able to run at speed to succeed at the 100 m sprint event.

25 Training zones

1 220 – Sunita's age (22) = 198 bpm.
2 For training in the aerobic training zone, Sunita's heart rate should be a minimum of 139 bpm (70 per cent) and a maximum of 158 bpm (80 per cent).

26 Fitness programme: gathering information

A PAR-Q assesses a participant's medical history. It is designed to help the sports/activity leader find out if the participant is well enough to take part in sport or activity, or whether they need a doctor's clearance or advice.

27 Programme design

1 Free weights, resistance machines.
2 Individual responses might vary. Answers could include:
   - Set the training at the correct level of intensity for Alex, e.g. size of weights used; number of reps and sets.
   - Recommend fixed resistance machines rather than free weights if Alex is new to strength training.
   - Make sure that Alex knows the correct technique for each exercise, to avoid the risk of injury.

28 Warm-up

Any two from: pulse raiser, mobiliser, stretch.

29 Main activities

1 20 minutes.
2 Sport-specific drills (isolated practice, travel, unopposed drills, opposed drills, pressurised drills); adapted game.

30 Cool down

Individual responses might vary: the participant could gradually decrease how quickly they are jogging, from fast to slow and then to walking.

31 Healthy diet

1 Adult males: 2500 kcal.
2 Adult females: 2000 kcal.

32 Carbohydrates

1 Simple and complex.
2 Any one from: wholegrain breakfast cereals, wholewheat pasta, wholemeal bread, brown rice, oats, vegetables, nuts, seeds.

33 Benefits of carbohydrates

The body doesn't have enough carbohydrate stores to supply the energy required to keep running during a marathon, as this event takes more than 90 minutes. Simple carbohydrates can be broken down very quickly by the body, so consuming simple carbohydrates during the event will provide energy for the marathon runner to keep exercising at a moderate to moderately high intensity.

34 Protein

1 Any two of the following: makes up the structure of the body; for growth (of children/of muscles as a result of exercise); repair of body tissues.
2 An essential amino acid is one that has to be consumed in the diet as the body is not able to make it.

35 Benefits of protein

Consuming protein foods straight after exercise helps to repair the muscle tissue at a faster rate than if is consumed much later after the activity.

36 Fats

Saturated fats contain cholesterol, which can build up in the walls of the arteries. The arteries become narrower, and this increases the risk of coronary heart disease.

37 Vitamins

1 Vitamin A helps to maintain normal eyesight.
2 Any one from: liver, mackerel, milk products, carrots, spinach.
3 Any one from: Vitamin B1, Vitamin C.

38 Minerals

Iron is needed in the diet to produce red blood cells. A triathlete takes part in aerobic activity, so they need to ensure they have enough red blood cells to carry oxygen around the body.

39 Hydration

1 2 litres (+ 1 additional litre for every hour of exercise)
2 Individual responses might vary. Any one answer from:
   - It helps to maintain body temperature: the fluid allows us to sweat, which helps prevent the body from overheating when taking part in sport and activity.
   - It lubricates the joints, allowing them to move freely.
   - It makes the blood plasma thinner, so it can work effectively and transport oxygen and nutrients to the muscles during sport and activity.

40 Sports nutrition

1 Individual answers could include triathlon, marathon, Tour de France cycling.
2 The body can only store enough carbohydrate to last for up to two hours of exercise. Carbohydrate loading increases the body's carbohydrate stores, and this helps supply energy for sports events lasting more than two hours.

41 Timing of food intake

Soraya should eat foods containing protein to repair the micro-tears in her muscles caused by weight training.

42 Legal supplements

Individual responses might vary.

Advantages – any one from:
- Caffeine can increase energy levels.
- It can increase alertness.
- It reduces a person's perception of effort when they are taking part in sport or activity.
- It increases the use of fats as an energy source.

Disadvantages – any one from insomnia, anxiety, diarrhoea, high blood pressure, energy peaks and troughs.

43 Motivation

1 Intrinsic.
2 A tangible reward is a physical reward such as prize money or a trophy.

44 Benefits of increased motivation

Individual responses might vary. Any two from:
- Players will put in a high intensity of effort during participation.
- Players will continue to take part on a regular basis.
- Players will be able to overcome adversity and keep playing.
- Players will have higher enjoyment levels.
- Players will experience increased intrinsic and extrinsic rewards.

45 Self-confidence

1 Self-confidence means the belief that a desired behaviour can be performed/having trust in yourself and believing in your own ability to achieve your goals.
2 Having high levels of self-confidence can help to improve Sanjay's performance because he will believe he is capable of performing at a high level. Because Sanjay feels that he is capable of doing well, he will be an active member of the rugby team.

46 Increasing self-confidence

Individual responses will vary. Two examples:
Grace could find a training partner to go running with her, who is at the same level of fitness. This will help improve her self-confidence, as she won't be on her own and they can help each to progress.
Grace could set herself achievable goals, such as starting by alternating walking and running, then running a whole mile. This will improve her confidence, because she will be able to see that her fitness levels are improving.

47 Anxiety

Trait anxiety is part of a person's personality, and so the person will become anxious in many different situations.

48 Effects of anxiety

Individual responses might vary.
Somatic anxiety is where a person feels physical effects of anxiety in their body, such as muscle tension. Cognitive anxiety is where a person experiences psychological effects of anxiety, such as feeling worried.

49 Controlling anxiety

Individual responses might vary.
The music will help participants to relax. They will focus on the music that is familiar to them, and this will help them to feel that the class is suitable for them to participate in.

50 Your Component 2 exam

Your notes on the Component 2 exam, always referring to the latest Sample Assessment Material on the Pearson website for an indication of assessment details.

51 'State' and 'Name' questions

Any two from: continuous training, fartlek training, interval training.

52 'Identify' questions

Intensity.

53 'Give' questions

Individual responses might vary. Complex carbohydrates provide long-lasting energy for aerobic activities, and running a marathon is an aerobic activity.

54 'Calculate' questions

1 2500 calories.
2 Lower (200 calories lower).

55 'Describe' questions

Individual responses might vary, but your description of progressive overload should include the following points:
- Gradually increase the training intensity over a set period of time …
- … in order to improve a specific component of fitness.

56 'Explain' questions

Individual responses might vary, but your answer should include the following points:
- Iron is used for red blood cell production.
- Having more red blood cells will increase the oxygen-carrying capacity of the blood.
- This enhances aerobic performance during long-distance running by delivering more oxygen to the working muscles for energy production.

57 Multi-part questions

Individual responses might vary. Example answers:
a Health information.
b A health-screening questionnaire/PAR-Q.
Or
a Lifestyle information (such as activity levels/alcohol intake/ stress/diet/smoking/sleep).
b A lifestyle questionnaire.
Or
a Activity likes and dislikes.
b Lifestyle questionnaire/consulting/discussing with the client.
Or
a Client's main aim and objectives.
b By consulting/discussing with the client.

58–59 Planning your responses to longer-answer questions

Your plan might include notes on some of the following:
- Circuit training develops muscular endurance.
- Tom requires muscular endurance in his leg muscles, which need to be able to contract repeatedly to run the full distance of the 10 km race.
- The intensity for circuit training is too low – it should be in the aerobic training zone, which is 70–80 per cent of Max HR to develop muscular endurance.
- Anaerobic hill sprints are used to develop power.
- Power will be beneficial for a 10 km cross-country run if the course includes steep hills that Tom has to run up.
- Increasing his power will allow Tom to run at speed up the hills and be faster than other competitors.
- The intensity is not high enough, as anaerobic training should be at an intensity of 80–100 per cent of Max HR.
- Continuous training develops aerobic endurance.
- This is needed for Tom's cardiorespiratory system to be able to deliver oxygen and nutrients to his working muscles during the race.

- Having high levels of aerobic fitness will allow Tom to keep running at a fast pace for the duration of the cross-country race.
- The intensity is correct, as aerobic training should be at 70–80 per cent of HR Max to have a training effect.
- The training programme doesn't show the time for each training session. Tom needs to complete each training session for long enough to develop the appropriate component of fitness.
- The training programme doesn't indicate how progressive overload will be achieved. This could be achieved by increasing the time or resistance used in each training session over the six-week period.
- A training programme needs to include at least one rest day to avoid overtraining. Tom's programme includes just one rest day, which is appropriate as he is training for an important race in six weeks' time.

Summary:

- A well-planned training programme is very important to prepare Tom for the 10 km cross-country race.
- Continuous training, circuit training and anaerobic hill sprints are all good for improving the components of fitness that Tom needs.
- The intensity of the circuit training and hill sprint training needs to be increased so that Tom's muscular endurance and power improve.
- The time of each training session needs to be added to the programme, to make sure that adaptations will occur.
- The programme should indicate how progressive overload will be achieved.

60 'Discuss' questions

Individual responses will vary, but your answer might include the points included for the plan (see the answer to pages 58–59).

61–62 'Evaluate' questions

Individual responses will vary, but your answer might include some of the following points:
Methods that can be used to increase self-confidence include: training with a partner or someone of a similar ability; goal setting; self-talk; creating a positive environment; providing positive reinforcement.

Training with a partner of similar ability

Pros: This will help Alicia to see that she is at a similar level as another participant. Training and improving together will help to increase her confidence.
Cons: It might not be possible to find a partner who is of the same ability. If she has a training partner who is at a higher level than her, it could reduce her self-confidence even more.

Goal setting

This is where realistic goals for training sessions and training programmes are set.
Pros: Alicia should set short-term and long-term goals. Achieving short-term goals will increase her self-confidence as she will see that she is improving in her event.
Cons: If she does not meet the set goals, it will make her doubt her ability and reduce her self-confidence.

Self-talk

Pros: Alicia could use positive affirmations to reassure herself that she has what is needed to be successful in the competition. She could use self-talk during training sessions and also during the competition.
Cons: She might be too anxious in the competition to use self-talk, as this method requires focus and concentration. This might not be possible if she is worrying about the event and her competitors.

Other methods: Creating a positive environment and providing positive reinforcement are both good methods of increasing self-confidence. However, these methods depend on the coach or activity leader, so are outside Alicia's control.

Conclusion

Alicia could start by setting goals for her training, making sure that she sets SMART goals that are within her ability to achieve. She should also try to find a training partner to help achieve her goals, making sure that the partner is the same ability level as herself.
Self-talk will be a useful technique throughout her training, and particularly at the competition itself. Simple, positive statements such as 'You can do this!' and 'Come on!' will help Alicia believe that she can perform well during the race and so help improve her performance.

63–64 'Analyse' questions with stimulus material

Individual responses will vary. Your answer may include some of the following points:

Frequency

- Jan trains six times a week, which is sufficient to result in fitness gains. This is necessary as it provides sufficient progressive overload to develop the components of fitness required to improve Jan's gymnastics performance.
- She also has a rest day, which is important to allow her body to recover and adapt to the training. This will help her to avoid overtraining.

Intensity

- Intensity is how hard a person trains.
- It is important to work at the right intensity to train for both aerobic and anaerobic fitness.
- Jan will train at high intensity for power and strength. These are both anaerobic activities, and so should be carried out at high intensity to increase anaerobic fitness.
- For flexibility training, the intensity can be based on a scale of low/moderate/high. There is no specific heart rate or training zone in order to gain fitness adaptations for flexibility training.

Type

- Type is the component of fitness being trained or type of training.
- For each component of fitness, an appropriate type of training method is used to develop that component of fitness.
- Plyometrics and strength training should be performed for both upper and lower body. As a gymnast, Jan needs power and strength in her legs to be able to jump high, and also in her arms to push off from the vault.
- Static stretching can be performed alone, allowing Jan to carry out this training when it suits her best.

Time

- This is the amount of time that the participant will train for in each session.
- For each of the types of training method in Jan's programme, there is no set timeframe required to have training adaptations.
- Strength and power both require training for a timeframe that encourages progressive overload. This can be carried out using sets and reps with weights. The time Jan spends training in the training programme should be appropriate to develop both of these components of fitness.
- The 30-minute set for the flexibility session should be sufficient for Jan to stretch all the main muscles and muscle groups, to develop her flexibility.